TO :

Dr. Robert Stake

with sincere appreciation
for your efforts to improve
college and youth sports.

Phil Bailey
June 16, 1997

ATHLETICS AND ACADEME

AN ANATOMY OF ABUSES
AND A PRESCRIPTION FOR REFORM

Wilford S. Bailey
Taylor D. Littleton

AMERICAN COUNCIL ON EDUCATION
MACMILLAN PUBLISHING COMPANY
New York
COLLIER MACMILLAN CANADA
Toronto
MAXWELL MACMILLAN INTERNATIONAL
New York   Oxford   Singapore   Sydney

Macmillan Publishing Company
866 Third Avenue, New York, N.Y. 10022

Collier Macmillan Canada, Inc.
1200 Eglinton Avenue East, Suite 200
Don Mills, Ontario, M3C 3N1

Library of Congress Catalog Card Number: 90-41860

Printed in the United States of America

printing number
1 2 3 4 5 6 7 8 9 10

Library of Congress Cataloging-in-Publication Data
Bailey, Wilford S.
     Athletics and academe: an anatomy of abuses and a prescription for
reform / Wilford S. Bailey and Taylor D. Littleton.
         p.   cm. — (American Council on Education/ Macmillan series in
higher education)
     Includes bibliographical references and index.
     ISBN 0-02-897028-4
     1. College sports—United States. 2. Sports—United States—Corrupt   prac-
tices. 3. National Collegiate Athletic Association. I. Littleton, Taylor.   II.
American Council on Education. III. Title. IV. Series.
     GV351.B34   1991
     796'.07'173—dc20
                                                                        90-41860
                                                                        CIP

To
Harry M. Philpott
and
to
our families
who share our love for college sports

CONTENTS

Acknowledgments

We express appreciation to the Lilly Endowment, Inc., the Rockefeller Foundation, and the John and Mary Franklin Foundation for their generous support of the research and writing associated with this book.

The particular character and content of the book have been affected strongly by the cooperation and assistance through personal interviews of twenty-two current or former chief executive officers of NCAA member institutions across the country, representing all divisions and subdivisions, but most of them in Division I-A. Not only did every CEO approached grant our request for an interview; each permitted us to tape-record the discussion to assure accuracy in our use of the information provided, and all authorized the use of verbatim quotations from the recorded interviews with the assurance of complete confidentiality with respect to the identification of both the individual and the institution(s) with which the individual is (or had been) associated. Without the full cooperation of these leaders in higher education, their generous contribution of time and thoughtful consideration of the issues posed, this book would not have been possible. For that assistance we are deeply grateful, and we regret that we can only thank them as an anonymous group.

There are also several persons to whom we are much indebted for their helpful critique of sections of the manuscript as the book was in progress: Sharon Andrus, Joseph S. Boland, III, Jerry E. Brown, Thomas J. Frericks, Asa Green, Adriane LaPointe, Donna Lopiano, Barbara Mowat, Jeffrey Orleans, and Donald Sabo.

We also wish to thank Sue Glaze for valuable research assistance, Mary Waters for assembling the index, Rosemary Thorne and Sandra Ramey for preparation of the manuscript, and William C. Highfill and many staff members of the Ralph B. Draughon Library at Auburn University.

We also wish to pay tribute to our many predecessors who have written on the topics addressed in this book and whose contributions to assessment of the problems in intercollegiate athletics and prospects for meaningful reform have greatly widened our own perspectives.

Wilford S. Bailey
Taylor D. Littleton

Auburn University
Auburn, Alabama

Introduction

Most colleges and universities conduct their varsity sports programs in strict compliance with the policies of the institution and with the regulations of the relevant governing athletic organizations. Most coaches are honest and resist temptations to cheat in response to the ever-present pressures to win. Nevertheless, abuses in intercollegiate athletics, which are more widespread than even the intense publicity some cases have attracted in recent years would suggest, can be accurately characterized as an illness of higher education—a strange pathology that has persisted for a century, with features analogous to an endemic disease in the population.

As the natural history of any endemic disease illustrates, obtrusive outbreaks of this particular illness have evoked varying degrees of concern and response. The 1929 study of intercollegiate athletics by the Carnegie Foundation for the Advancement of Teaching is perhaps the most detailed and widely quoted of these responses. Until the recent past, there have been few other significant responses. Still, sixty years later the same problems, greatly magnified, persist and are exerting more deleterious effects on higher education than ever before.

There are many reasons for the lack of effective control of abuses in college sports. Perhaps the two most important are the failure of the leadership of higher education to recognize the seriousness of the problem and the fact that over the past century control has often been directed more toward treatment of the symptoms than to the fundamental causes of the malady, a phenomenon almost universally characteristic of reactions to clinical experience with an illness. As a result, the complex matrix of causes has not been adequately clarified, and, therefore, no foundation has been developed for a holistic approach to the control of abuses in college sports with emphasis on the fundamental causes.

To suggest that higher education is afflicted with something comparable to a terminal disease, a perception easily gained from sensational media reports, would be reckless exaggeration; but to affirm that it has a serious illness, a persistent pathology, cannot be denied. The fact that the great majority of colleges and universities are currently experiencing no serious ailment and that many have never had a conspicuous manifestation of this illness in no way diminishes the need for an analysis and prescription. The history of these particular abuses shows clearly that the "infection" is latent and persistent, with potential for severe damage. Complacency is fraught with danger when one attempts to address a disease that is often clinically silent and in which the manifestations of most cases are mild, but which has much potential for damage. This is particularly true in view of the fact that the prevalence is more widespread than is generally recognized, even in smaller colleges where the most highly publicized causes of problems are nonexistent.

Frequent reference is made in the text to the National Collegiate Athletic Association (NCAA) as a national organization for governance of intercollegiate athletics. There are two reasons for the specificity of reference to the NCAA: it is the "big-time" programs in the institutions that constitute Division I of the NCAA that historically have received the most publicity involving problems in college sports, and the authors' experiences have been limited to such an institution, to a conference comprised of Division I-A institutions, and to the NCAA organizational structure—its council, executive committee, and various standing and special committees.

It seems, however, logical that the same basic problems confronting NCAA member institutions also occur in the sports programs of other two-year and four-year colleges, which have their own governing organizations (e.g., the National Association of Intercollegiate Athletics). To the extent that this is true, the principles for analysis, diagnosis, and control of those problems would, it seems, therefore be applicable to the institutions that comprise those organizations. We do not presume to speak for those organizations and their member institutions but hope that the principles set forth in this narrative will be helpful to them as well as to the NCAA membership.

The diversity in the nature of violations of institutional policy or governing legislation is as great as that seen in the broad spectrum of disease. Most violations of NCAA regulations are minor ("secondary," as classified by that association and defined as "one that provides only a limited recruiting or competitive advantage and that is isolated or inadvertent in nature"). These are comparable to a mild illness such as the common cold. But conditions that predispose to minor ailments can, when allowed to persist, lead to more serious illness. Furthermore, a philosophy that accepts the occurrence of minor illness as normal and as no reason for concern can easily result in failure to recognize the early signs of serious illness, with the result that major corrective measures, analogous to surgery or prolonged intensive therapy, may be required.

For all these reasons, the language of medical metaphors, used throughout the text, provides an ideal approach for the analysis of the causes of abuses in intercollegiate athletics. From such an analysis an understanding of the nature and interrelationship of fundamental and contributing or secondary causes can be achieved, an accurate diagnosis can be made, and rational basis for effective control can be established.

In this narrative, an "abuse" is defined as (1) the abdication of institutional responsibility for the welfare of student-athletes, with the emphasis of that responsibility lying not only on requirements for admission and academic progress that assure for each one a meaningful education and strong probability for acquiring a degree but also on the noncurricular development of personal qualities that prepare any student for life beyond the university experience; (2) the failure of an institution to exercise appropriate controls in the administration of the athletic program, thus permitting violations to occur; or (3) any intentional violation of institutional policies or conference or national regulations governing the conduct of intercollegiate athletics. From this definition, it should be obvious that minor infrequent or inadvertent violations are not considered to be abuses, but the failure of an institution to put in place appropriate controls to prevent the continuing recurrence of such violations would constitute an abuse.

This book is divided into five sections. The first, "Case History," shows how the forces of American culture have contributed to the development of the unique representational identity intercollegiate athletics have acquired as a part of higher education in our nation. It is in this relationship that the interrelated fundamental and contributing causes of abuses in college sports have found an environment conducive not only to their persistence, but to activities producing frequent eruptive disorders.

The second section, titled "Diagnosis: The Pathology of Infractions," begins with a brief discussion of the signs of overt illness, based on selected data from an analysis of the penalties imposed by the NCAA since the initiation of its enforcement program in 1952. This is followed by a detailed discussion of the causes of abuses in college sports, both fundamental and contributing, with emphasis on the interrelationship of these causes, in the context of the concept of "multifactorial etiology of disease" (a concept of latent infection and exciting causes of illness), a term that is clarified in the text as the defining metaphor of analysis.

The third section, "Prescription for Reform: The Essential Ingredients," begins with a brief discussion of alternative strategies for achieving and maintaining a relationship between athletics and education that is mutually supportive. The remainder of the section addresses in detail various elements of what, at this juncture, is viewed as the only viable alternative: reform of the traditional structure. Primary emphasis is placed on control at the institutional level, but with the recognition that this can be accomplished only with the cooperation of partners of the institution—a conference (when there is such affiliation) and the NCAA, along with the support of other entities such as national educational organizations and the media. Detailed attention is given to the proper roles of the following in the discussion of control at the institutional level: governing board, chief executive officer, faculty, director of athletics, coach, student-athletes, and alumni (fans).

The fourth section, "Prescription Refinement: Improving the Prognosis," makes the point that in order to achieve a meaningful reform of college sports major changes must be made in national governing legislation, changes that will help in spanning the fissure that exists between athletics and education in an increasing number of colleges and universities. Selected areas of legislation, of which there is no better example than recruiting, are discussed to illustrate the breadth and complexity of these issues on which national consensus for change must be achieved.

In the fifth section, "In the Waiting Room: The Prospect for Wholeness," the medical metaphor is completed by emphasizing the present uncertainty of the outcome—whether meaningful reform will be achieved, and the social and psychological consequences attendant on failure. If reform is to come about, a wholeness must be established in the relationship between athletics and academe. Without that wholeness, integrity in intercollegiate athletics is a mirage. The prognosis for reform, however, is more favorable than in recent memory, possibly more than in the past century, because there is now a better understanding of the nature and scope of the problem and its causes and a growing public consciousness of the effects of abuses on the quality of higher education. Too, there is a more apparent willingness of academe and society generally to face these realities of the illness and its consequences. This book is a statement of belief that the outcome—still very uncertain—can be positive.

Chapter 1

Case History

April 4, 1989. The last game of the Final Four is nearing its close. One of the teams on the floor represents one of the nation's largest and most prestigious research universities, which, in a few months, will send its football team to the Rose Bowl; the other team, not well known nationally, is from a school less than half as large and essentially limited in its academic and athletic reputations to the urban northeast. That these two teams could be competitively engaged at this supreme level illustrates the democratic character of the only significant athletic game created by Americans. For a brief moment the conversation of the two television commentators turns to one of the finest players in the contest, widely known to be a member of another country's Olympic team, who is playing only this year in the United States before returning to that competition. One of the analysts asks the other if such a situation "is good for the game." "Well," comes the reply, "it's within the rules."

That reply is notable. Some observers in the vast audience might reflect on the irony, even the humor, of an intercollegiate championship game being strongly influenced by the play of the subject of this conversation. But they would be few indeed. Our games have always been taken too seriously for them to appear either contradictory or amusing. And besides, there are probably many examples, though perhaps not as dramatic, throughout intercollegiate sports similar to this one. But the reply is notable too in that it reaches back, in a sense, into the history of sports in America, defining some of the relationships to the national life that they assumed early in their existence and that they still essentially retain.

In fact, this last game of the season itself contains the hard residue of these relationships, sharing them with the other major intercollegiate sport in our country, which, unlike basketball, originated in nineteenth-century England, but which was significantly altered after being imported to America. While the cultural distance between Victorian England and the last Final Four contest of the 1980s may seem considerable, we can now perceive, on the strength of much recent historical scholarship, that many of our intercollegiate games began to flourish, and subsequently to develop as spectator encounters, as a kind of extension of the work world of modern industrial society. Today they are marked in their presentation by the qualities characteristic of that 150-year continuum: emphases on efficiency and measurement, rewards for the attainment of new production records, the evolution of rapid systems of transportation and communication, and, of course, the tendency toward codification of enforceable rules that themselves shape and regulate organizational patterns.[1]

The model of Victorian English sport, with its emphasis on games as ends in themselves and governed by an ideal conception of "sportsmanship" more important than "the rules," never really had a chance in America. The absence of a secure and recognized class to sustain and reenforce such a system accounted in part for that, of course. But the rapidly evolving forms of existence in a frontier society gradually accommodating itself to an industrialized economy simply would not permit its sports and games ultimately to be exempt from a pragmatic role in a country that was consciously starting over, rejecting its potential inheritance of English or European traditions or finding that they "wouldn't work" in the new setting.

No less an observer than Charles Dickens, who had visited America in the early 1840s, caught this sense of evolutionary haste and rejection. In *The Life and Adventures of Martin Chuzzlewit* (1844), the only one of his novels with an American setting, Dickens has his English hero interview such citizens as the editor of the *New York Rowdy Journal*, where he is informed not only that "We are an elastic country" but also one where the sun shines perennially, as it rarely does in England. Though such sentiments as these occur in the midst of the caricatures of such American "institutions" as the Eden Land Corporation, they nevertheless find a serious and substantial affirmation in the convictions of the young Walt Whitman, who was in those years about to begin work on what would become the most significant poem in the literature of the new nation and whose preface would extol the poem's "audacity of freedom necessary to loosen the mind of still-to-be-form'd America" from the "stifling anti-democratic" cultures of the past.[2]

By the time an expanded *Leaves of Grass* had reached a second edition in 1856, the British style and spirit of such imported sports as yachting and horse racing were already on the wane, and within two decades or so the aspirations of cricket to become the national game would be in sharp decline. And in 1880, only two or three years before the creator of Huckleberry Finn was making plans for his hero "to light out for the Territory," where in its open, unstructured landscapes he could escape the restraints of "sivilization," Walter Camp introduced at Yale changes in the sport of football—replacing the rugby scrum with the scrimmage, setting the number of players at eleven—which further altered the game into a contest between two organized units with emphasis on the strategy that could be devised within the rules. In fact, five years earlier, with the establishment of a championship game among the members of the Intercollegiate Football Association, emphasis in this particular sport was permanently shifted from the inherited conception of how one played to which team won. Although it would be folly to oversimplify the matter and state that the ideal of British "sportsmanship" disappeared in these formative years of college sports, nevertheless the two principal intercollegiate games that subsequently flourished in America have not generally been marked by the philosophy of pride-in-failure-of-a-game-well-played. As testimony to this, once the present contest is over, one has only to observe the genuinely agonized and downcast expressions of the Seton Hall players as they accept the handshakes of their Michigan opponents.

Gradually, then, intercollegiate games—and their professional successors—were systematically ordered into patterns of activity enclosed by rules against which teams had to contend in order to win. The innovative tactic of signal calling, for example, introduced in the early 1880s by the Yale football team as a means of strategically confusing its opponents, appears as an extended connection in the decision of a college coach one hundred years later who, in the heat of a big game, calls consecutive time-outs in order to put pressure on the opponent's player at the free-throw line. This early but steady emphasis in the developing world of sport on gamesmanship—securing a competitive advantage "within the rules"—finds a strange correlation with the assertive freedom of Whitman's verse and Huck's hasty departure for the frontier territory. Each in its own way is symbolic of a certain form of emancipation, a response in this developing "elastic" nation to inherited traditions both social and literary. Mark Twain himself, of course, as well as many of his twentieth-century successors, would both assess and criticize in various ways the unashamedly mercantile dimension of American life, which Dickens had perceived earlier as a self-conscious force in the shaping of a new kind of society. But it was in the games that began to emerge on college campuses and sandlot diamonds throughout the nation that this society eventually discovered in a popular and binding identity some of its most significant symbolic qualities: organizational efficiency; an emphasis on winning, which accommodates the democratic tendency to measure and record achievement; and, above all perhaps, the energetic participation of young people, whose sustaining and transient presence suggests that failure can never be permanent. In America, there is always next season.

This power of games in assigning gradually a certain degree of symbolic unity to the aggressive and dislocated culture Dickens had caricatured in the 1840s appears almost unexpectedly some eighty years later in the equally perceptive observations of another English novelist. Writing in 1925 in high praise of Ring Lardner, the only significant American writer to use sports as an important fictional setting, Virginia Woolf clearly saw that the English style, with its class consciousness and reverential sense of the past, could never have coped with the immensity of the American landscape, its enormous industrial cities with "their night signs and their perfect organization of machinery." And she saw too that it was no accident that Lardner's best work was about games, which had "given him a clue, a centre, a meeting place for the divers activities of people whom a vast continent isolates, whom no tradition controls." That Lardner's principal game was baseball is less important than the fact that in writing about it, especially in *You Know Me, Al*, with its slangy account of the innocent boastful athletic-hero playing his sport in a rowdy spectacle across the American scene, Lardner had captured a kind of authenticity—"a society," Woolf concluded, "which goes its way intent on its own concerns," finding in its games a certain native coherence.[3]

That coherence is intensely represented by the game we are watching on the television screen. It is the climax of what is perhaps the most extraordinary public display of democratic organization and efficiency outside the functions of the state itself: a tournament of sixty-four teams representing universities of all shapes and sizes, chosen by a process that combines specific rules and subjective judgment with sophisticated computerized ratings. These teams have played their games literally across the span of the nation in both collegiate and metropolitan arenas. This final game has been placed in "prime time"—that is, presumably, when most of America is not working and thus has time to watch—and is being partly communicated to the audience in terms of an almost bewildering array of statistics. Through its network of corporate sponsorships the game illustrates also the assertion by the business-industrial community of its claims on this dimension of the nation's cultural life—and within a few months the television contract for the tournaments of the 1990s will pose for the NCAA the peculiar problem of distributing properly an amount of wealth unimaginable in the 1970s.

Finally, this climactic game of a sport invented to be played indoors during the cold winter months is taking place on an April evening, weeks after the good presence of spring has appeared in the land. (The professional version will not conclude until June!) This maximizing of what might commercially be described as a production-consumption pattern for goods and services, a pattern that annually of course is replicated in the sports of football and baseball, may well have confused slightly the connection between our collegiate sports and the natural rhythms of the year to which they were once more closely attuned. But the extension of a sport's "season" is only a response, as production always is, to a demand for an increase of whatever qualities these games represent.[4]

There are, clearly, limits to the metaphorical uses of the Michigan-Seton Hall game and the brief dialogue between television commentators Billy Packer and Brent Musburger. Yet those uses should not be construed as merely clinical or descriptive. Though this particular game is now over, it will of course be re-born in another season. And then, too, it will continue to reflect many of the characteristics it absorbed from the scientific-industrial society along with which it grew, and to display as well that quality of independent self-absorption, which Virginia Woolf so aptly observed from her transatlantic stance, that America had gradually achieved. "Within the rules" is thus a phrase at once richly suggestive of both the evolution and at least a portion of the symbolic place that games, especially intercollegiate games, have assumed in our country's life.

Despite this context, however, the relatively mild query about "what's good for the game" has persisted with increasing intensity throughout the 1980s. The decade has been framed, in a sense, by two bold and angry assertions from prominent writers in *Sports Illustrated*, the principal journal of the sports establishment: one, that intercollegiate sports, especially football and basketball, are reft with corruption, hypocrisy, and sordidly misplaced values, and the other, that those who supposedly have authority over such matters are doing nothing about it even though the scandals are plainly visible and thoroughly documented.[5] Challenges to the accuracy of this alleged condition of shame and disgrace have been noticeably absent. And who is to say that reluctance to confront a kind of cultural shock has not been the reason for our relative paralysis in diagnosing and treating what can only be described as a social illness. There is a slowly dawning sense, on the one hand, that the current condition of college sports is directly related to their excessive assimilation of the very qualities that, as we have briefly seen, have made them somehow representative of the society that they both entertain and unite in subtle and complex ways. And, on the other hand, there is apparently now a disquieting awareness that this excessive emphasis on winning and setting new records combined with the deep involvement of intercollegiate athletics in a commercial pattern of production-consumption-marketing of services have placed them in an ethical stance directly opposed to that of the institutions that gave them their life.

> *Most of our college games developed in society and came onto the campus, baseball included. But our two most important games—the energy of the system—are different. Football and basketball grew up on the campus, they weren't imported; and they've just gotten beyond effective control and now are damaging the image of the institution. Their problems embarrass us in the same way the reverse of that is true —they bring us some moments of joy and pleasure, but neither of those touch the intrinsic value and work of the institution.[6]*

That the regulation, as this university president states, of college sports has gotten "beyond effective control" and that unethical practices in the recruitment and treatment of student athletes have begun to damage the reputation of higher education are both emphasized by the bleak prospect contained in current congressional hearings that in the 1990s the state will begin to monitor and influence the whole arrangement. This depressing intrusion may come about even if higher education should initiate genuinely meaningful reforms that would at least partially redeem the strained connection between sport and university. Some dramatic action appears inevitable and the application of a series of procedural band-aids will not significantly conceal or modify an infected condition that is neither localized nor of recent origin.

Only in the United States, of course, have athletics assumed such a close and representational identity with higher education. But almost from the time that intercollegiate sports first appeared, they have never escaped the charges that their self-fulfilling character, their inherent professionalism, and their primary purpose of providing entertainment have made their presence contradictory to the educational goals of the university. The current inseparability of sports, especially football, from the infrastructure of higher education was prefigured late in the previous century in the building of expensive stadiums on college property—inevitably with borrowed funds to be repaid from spectator charges, the frequent playing of championship games in metropolitan centers, and the increasingly widespread coverage of games by newspaper and later by radio.[7] For it was only when the sporting scene began to move, emotionally and at times literally, beyond the confines of the college playing field that the social and populist linkages were formed that gave intercollegiate contests a security their intrinsic character could never have sustained.

Perhaps as much as any aspect of American life, this form of sport accommodated itself to that sense of elasticity and rapid momentum that Dickens had observed on his midcentury visits. Like the new nation, sports never looked back, always improving their technique, equipment, and organization. And as college athletics extended themselves to wider and wider audiences with new technologies, they gradually formed one of those real but less chartered fellowships that would eventually rival the older, inherited ones of religion and politics, holding Americans together, as Daniel J. Boorstin would write, "by countless gossamer webs knitting together the trivia of their lives."[8]

Though sports have always readily accepted from their defenders and apologists the argument that their presence within the university can be justified solely on their character-building capability, that thesis has long since run its course.[9] Actually, it was never really needed, for sports through their popular and ceremonial appeal to alumni could serve—and do still—as a core of identity and remembrance, their stadiums and coliseums bearing names and symbolic decorations of past triumphs that consecrate both field and court in ways impossible of application to classrooms or laboratories. Sports assumed, against criticisms of their contradictory presence and questionable value, a kind of independence and polite defiance as to their importance and uniqueness, not unlike that confidence expressed in the laconic reply of Babe Ruth to Calvin Coolidge's complaint that the Babe made more money than he did: "I had a better year than him." Though it is impossible to find a precise beginning for cultural extensions of this complexity, it might be observed that from the moment in 1878 when the Yale faculty voted to excuse from recitations members of the football team so they could participate in an intercollegiate game, the prerogatives of organized athletics have steadily challenged those of the academy. Historically, the ability of sports to align themselves with current social and cultural realities at a vastly more rapid pace than universities either could or were willing to do has only served to strain further the relationship.

College sports have, of course, almost always been our common property—especially since the advent of television, assimilating, as we have seen, in their organization, technological projection to consumer masses, and financial linkages with the corporate world of business, entertainment, and advertising many of the elements that are implicit in the life of modern American society. Universities, conversely, in their sometimes inscrutable style of organization and procedure and in their conservative curricular patterns remain among the least scrutinized of our social institutions. And, despite their enormously sophisticated research uses of science and technology, their corresponding commitment to capture and retain a vision of the past has given them, to many, an intrinsically archaic dimension, one rather remote from social immediacy. Thus the relationship between college sports and their containing environment, which one hundred years ago began as mere discomfort, has now become in reality a sharply divided double culture, forming—in most institutions, as the following pages will illustrate—an uneasy coexistence always subject to ethical confrontation. Efforts to ameliorate this condition by the university's asserting its academic prerogatives are often met by strident and protesting voices.[10]

> *When you have read about coaches being quoted, coming out publicly against their university presidents on academic principles, I can tell you that would have been unheard of twenty-five years ago, absolutely unheard of!*

The continuing rivalry and, by implication, the ultimate collision between what might be called the prevailing value systems of sports and the university have not, by any means, historically gone unnoticed, such notices largely coming, however, from academic sources and very few from professional sports journalists. The two most comprehensive surveys of this relationship appear some forty-five years apart, each at the observing end of a great surge in popularity of intercollegiate athletics. Both are essentially addressed to an academic-professional readership and neither led to any substantive reforms. Yet it is at least interesting to note, especially as we continue to learn, and to suspect, more about the psychic connection between our games—especially intercollegiate athletics—and our ordinary lives, that each report appeared at a significant moment of stress in the national experience: in the year of the stock market crash of 1929, and in 1974, the year in which the nation watched a president resign his office.

A report of the Carnegie Foundation for the Advancement of Teaching[11] addressed in an alternate mode the pervasive theme that F. Scott Fitzgerald, the most representative American novelist of the 1920s, had developed in his work: the corrupting power of money. And though the order of magnitude is different, there may be more than a fanciful affinity between the minor but powerfully symbolic character who appears in *The Great Gatsby*—the man who fixed the 1919 World Series—and the compromised university environment that the Carnegie report identified as the result of the commercialization of college sports, their attendant luxury, and the disproportionate place they had assumed in higher education. The brief allusion in the novel to the Black Sox scandal does not necessarily in any apocalyptic way anticipate the ultimate imprisonment in their own wealth of professional sports in the 1980s: the lockouts, the bargaining tables, the scab seasons (Babe Ruth's value judgment we have long since taken for granted). Rather, the detail suggests the larger social background, within which the national pastime has been bought and sold, against which Fitzgerald's tragic story of the sterility of wealth, unresponsive lives, and flawed American ideals is played out.

But *The Great Gatsby* was published in 1925, the same year, we might recall, in which Virginia Woolf made her perceptive observation about the milieu of American games and their connection with our national sense of disengagement from past traditions. And one short but unerring phrase in the novel suggests a further stage in this irregular "case history" as collegiate sports, especially football, gradually began to rival, essentially to displace, professional baseball as the game whose noisy spectacle and connection to personally remembered conjunctions of time and place seemed most capable of bringing its viewers into one of the new American fellowships. The rich, insensitive, and destructive Tom Buchanan, wrote Fitzgerald at the close of the story, "would drift on forever seeking, a little wistfully, for the dramatic turbulence of some irrecoverable football game," a vague quest not only revealing his one attractive feature but also suggesting a wider meaning of the collegiate game as a dynamic, coherent structure remotely juxtaposed to the disarray and aimlessness of Tom's life.[12] There is no hint, of course, in the Carnegie report of this kind of suggestive symbolism that collegiate games might eventually encompass: an image that publicly reveals the life of our democratic design "within the rules" of a structure whose self-contained integrity may assume an ironic relationship to the "trivia" of our daily existence. That conception would continue to grow as college sports became more visible and American life increasingly homogenized. However, the postwar period of prosperity, newfound leisure, and increased national prestige undoubtedly did hasten the translation of college sports into a new and bright symbol of vigorous promise and unifying capability.

Looking back now from a perspective of more than sixty years, one has to be slightly surprised at the tone of ethical outrage in the Carnegie report, for there is little, if any, evidence to indicate that during the 1920s, unlike the 1980s, there was extensive public recognition that intercollegiate sports—or professional sports, despite the 1919 scandal—were being infiltrated by corrupting forces. Notably, however, the report was composed only three years after *The Great Gatsby* appeared and was itself published in the same year as *The Sun Also Rises*, the other principal novel of the decade. And as we continue to seek connections between our intercollegiate games and the wider life of the culture, it is difficult to overlook in the report's urgent assessment of the corrupted relationship between college sports and the university setting that pervasive sense of lost innocence and self-doubt that both Fitzgerald and Hemingway portray as signs of the time.

The perilous condition of college sports seemed, in 1929, to be a microcosm of the instability of what the Carnegie report regarded as a "period of rapid industrial and social adjustment" through which the nation was then passing. And all of the ills then inherent in that condition, which had not yet "received the scrutiny that is their due," but were specifically described in the report have reappeared publicly and uneasily in our own recent past:

- The materialistic impulse transmitted through the university by the erection of an opulent athletic power structure
- The commercial extension of the student-athlete program into the domain of advertising and public relations
- The reluctance of university leadership to take unpopular stands and "bring athletics into a sincere relation" to the academic purposes of the institution
- The sordid system of subsidized recruitment, in which alumni often take part—"the most disgraceful phase of recent intercollege athletics"
- The professional nature of the student-athlete's duty ("it is work, not play") and the extreme difficulty of his balancing the time and energy requisite to that duty against academic responsibilities
- The unfortunate message sent to secondary schools of the exaggerated place of athletics in higher education

and, perhaps most significant of all,

- The growth both within and without the university of a cynical and tainted environment in which the effects of a "demoralizing and corrupt system" proceed "alike for the boy who takes the money and for the agent who arranges it, and for the whole group of college and secondary schools boys who know about it"

It is not clear, of course, from the report how much its level of social consciousness was elevated by the unsettling perception that intercollegiate sports were not innocently remote from contamination and that the citadel of higher education itself was being blemished in the process—and indeed was even partly responsible for the situation. Nor is it clear more than sixty years later how much our sense of anger and futility about the corruption of college sports is related to a suppressed awareness of our own complicity in sustaining and tolerating this condition. Already in the 1920s higher education was becoming a means toward upward social mobility and thus acquiring its peculiar and frustrating vulnerability of having its basic educational purposes and sense of academic integrity obscured by eager public judgments of its social utility. Thus, in retrospect, the primary importance of this relatively minor document, whose message was soon lost in the wake of Black Tuesday, is that—from the perspective of an earlier decade uncomfortably similar to that in which we live now—it tells us simply that the hypocrisy of college sports and their contradictory challenge of the values held by their sponsoring body were not then matters of public concern.

As we look back at the report as a kind of signpost in our reluctant national quest to confront and resolve the destructive tension between athletics and academe, we see that it also reveals, perhaps for the first time and perhaps unconsciously, the central dilemma inherent in that relationship: the unavoidable conclusion that higher education cannot control the cultural forces into which college sports have evolved and are evolving still. Their linkage with the corporate state now obviously prevails at a level inconceivable in the 1920s, and there can be little argument that their psychic claim on the national imagination is one more of dependence than occasional relief:

Think about it for a minute. There's very little that this state does very well, in which it really excels—and I believe there are more like ours than are not. I think that's why a football or a basketball program in many sections of the country is so crucial. Maybe it makes up for something. But our state needs _____ basketball on Saturday night. It's symbolically larger than life.

How much the nation—or how much of the nation—*needs* college sports to deliver a reassuring core of ritual meaning ordinarily unavailable in our daily life can never be clear. But what is clear is that few universities, public and private, now are free from the rather intimidating although perhaps unintentional hold their athletic programs have on them. Even the few whose academic emphases either predate the dramatic evolution of college sports or in some other way avoided an overt relationship feel the pressure of those forces that can lead to an academic-athletic imbalance and thus to abuses of the kind with which this book is concerned.

It would be suicide, literally suicide, for us to allow our academic program to decline in favor of athletics. We could not survive. Naturally, we are pleased with the success of our intercollegiate sports and we know for a fact that they create a visibility for the institution, but if we were to let it go at that and be recognized only for athletics, I'm sure the university would go into a serious decline.

As we shall see later, no institution—including the one to which this CEO referred, with its fine perspective—can escape the threat of ethical disruption that lies latent in the separated condition between the body of higher education and its athletic subculture. Because of the positive visibility and consolidation of loyalties that even a modestly successful athletic program can engender ("It's sure easier to ask about university financial support when you've won a ball game than when you've lost," says one CEO), universities are continually vulnerable to their own self-generated pressures to enhance athletics.

You see we're not there, at the top of the rung and we have such divided athletic expectations—those alums of twenty years ago can't wait to reclaim the glory years, but our recent graduates just never had that experience, and one of our real worries is who's going to help support the program? Our attendance figures for our twenty-five-to-thirty-five-year-old alumni are not nearly what they would be at schools with a more winning tradition. It really worries us; we're having meetings now on how we can get those people really sold on the university.

And, of course, the university now, significantly more than in 1929, must accommodate those particular alumni and supporters for whom the faculty voice in the classroom indeed has not necessarily been forgotten, or for whom the institution's life-improving results of research have not gone unrecognized, but whose interest and vanity have turned them toward what they perceive to be—and what, in fact, is—for the majority of contemporary universities the most public and culturally prestigious expression of identity. The erection in the last twenty-five years of egocentric and financial power structures around intercollegiate football or basketball programs, together with what still appears to be a public absorption with the university's utilitarian value, has made it virtually impossible for much of higher education to maintain in critical suspension the rival values and orientations of athletics and academe. Yet, though each seems to regard the evidence as inadmissible, both need the other for their separate existence and level of identity.

Historically, the emerging signs of anxiety about the corruption of college sports that appeared in the 1929 Carnegie report seem to have been temporarily held off by the binding experiences of the Depression and World War II. And we should be somehow grateful for the image of hope and social assimilation that intercollegiate athletics and sports at other levels as well held out to the nation in the midst of those sacrificial and disciplinary years. The heroic exploits recorded on the sports pages were welcome contrasts to the gloomy economic and political news described elsewhere; and, of course, during the war many of the very best football players drew military assignments to Annapolis and West Point, the academy teams becoming highly visible symbols of America's strength and virility. Less noticeable but perhaps even more important during the period were those multiple dramas of ethnic and class integration that took place on hundreds of college and high school gridirons and baseball diamonds and that were an early prelude to the collegiate accommodation of race and gender into athletic programs some thirty years later. Television would later extend the growing fellowship of intercollegiate sports throughout the wide fields of the republic. But during the 1930s and the war years these democratic reconciliations, though socially significant, were either relatively silent or set forth in scores of fictional accounts where players from both sides of the tracks would discover a grudging mutuality of respect and purpose in the stress of an American Legion baseball tournament; where a Jewish, Italian, or black football player would nobly suffer through discriminatory treatment and by his courage and athletic prowess win the hearts of the student body; or where, as aptly named in one story, "The Kid from Hard-Knocks U" would appear in many versions, sometimes as a "tramp" athlete, who would lose his cynicism and find a meaningful personal redemption by his participation in the trials of a small college football team.

The coach of that team was probably fatherly, ethically incorruptible, and had an attractive daughter who was an undergraduate English major. But the romance of college sports and the concept of the game as a significant moment of trial did seem to survive relatively untouched into the enormous release of social energy after the war, when many expressions of the culture such as art, literature, and technology were finding new forms of expression highly confrontational to those inherited from the 1930s. To be sure, the gambling scandals in college basketball during the 1950s may assign a brief cultural linkage between intercollegiate athletics and the short life of the *film noir*, movies of the period that, despite the marquee proclamation "Gable's Back and Garson's Got Him," dramatized realistic scenes of urban crime and corruption in the postwar setting. This actuality in sports was potentially a disturbing sign of their continuing vulnerability to the inevitable compromises attendant on commercial intrusions. But such a sign was less relevant to the time than the essentially democratic image revealed in almost every play or score in a football or basketball game: the success or failure of the transcendent individual gesture depending on the support and cohesion of the team itself—an image rather opposed to that depicted in the most influential social interpretation of the decade, David Riesman's *The Lonely Crowd* (1950), where individual effort for survival in bureaucratic organizations was seen as continually frustrated and suppressed by the dominating cultivation of "teamwork."[13]

As we have seen, the forms and uses of games, especially the major intercollegiate games, have over a century provided subtle, sometimes indirect, and often ironic comments on the course and stages of our national life.   For example, it is only a historical accident, though certainly an interesting one, that the forward pass, which essentially brought the game of football into the modern era, was introduced during the same year that Ring Lardner wrote the stories published later as *You Know Me, Al*, the book on which Virginia Woolf primarily based her judgment about American games and their connection with our feeling of independence and isolated self-absorption. But this was also the year in which the Great War was initiated in a remote European country, drawing America reluctantly but inevitably out of that secure sense of enclosure. Ten years later, one of the two young men, then a coach at his alma mater, who had participated in the forward pass innovation introduced into the Notre Dame backfield the "shift," a maneuver that would baffle opponents and carry the Irish to the Rose Bowl. The fluid choreography of the shift may have been in 1924 less than the Charleston a visual representation of the social dislocations and frenzied uses of wealth whose chronicle even then Fitzgerald was definitively completing in *The Great Gatsby*, and which would be identified in four years by the Carnegie report as relevant to the corruption of college sports. But for our purposes Coach Knute Rockne's brilliant innovative tactic of the shift illustrates, again, how within a structured limitation the "rules of the game" could be stretched to that very limit for an advantage. And perhaps it illustrates too, less distinctly but still visibly in a symbolic sense, that in 1924 Notre Dame football—and by extension all of our intercollegiate games—can be seen as a stable image of freedom and containment set against an "elastic" society not unlike that earlier one confronted by the English visitor Charles Dickens, but a society that would this time within five years stretch disastrously beyond its own limits.

The ills that continue to plague college sports as the decade of the 1990s begins are essentially those identified in the Carnegie report of 1929 and which were reconfirmed in 1974 by the appearance of an outline sponsored by the American Council on Education (ACE) for a national inquiry into the state of intercollegiate athletics.[14] The total study projected in the latter report was not completed but even in its preliminary form it serves as the second principal document on the subject. Its stated purpose was not to condemn but rather to identify ways in which intercollegiate athletics could be strengthened. The ACE document is valuable not only in its affirmation of the fissure lying between the goals and values of higher education and college sports, but also in its perception that the education and concern for the welfare of the student athletes is of secondary interest in many big-time athletic programs. As we shall discuss later, this concern is directly connected to the widespread erosion of academic and admission standards in the difficult years of student protests in the 1960s, and though much of that educational disarray is now laid to rest, its effect on intercollegiate athletics not only lingers still but seriously inhibits measures of reform.

Although in its tone of judicious restraint the ACE document exhibits no connection to the ethical crisis of the Watergate years, it was in fact distributed to the ACE membership only six weeks before that crisis reached its conclusion. At the present time, however, any consideration of an erosion of faith in the integrity of intercollegiate athletics must inevitably find a depressing correspondence in the wider context of public dismay and frustration that accompanied the revelations of that earlier period and that have persisted throughout the 1980s. In an essay written in the same year that the ACE report was in preparation, historian Barbara Tuchman addressed what seemed to be then our cynical loss of confidence in the sources of authority: "Who believes today in the integrity of government?—or of business, or of law or justice or labor unions or the military or the police?"[15] And, as our willingness (need?) to confront the relationship between sport and university has accelerated, we can perceive in the continuing recent history of deception and covert action in government (as described by Bill Moyers on public television) unsettling parallels in the way the affairs of our athletic programs often seem to be secretly conducted: laws are OK, but they constrain the practical action it takes to *win*—"we know what it's like out there"; sometimes illegality is absolutely necessary to protect America in the "real world"—"one just can't tell everyone about these things."[16] Within this context the good and forthright efforts of numerous coaches, faculty, university administrators, alumni, and supporters to maintain an open and honest environment are continually eroded by a kind of ethical dulling of our senses:

> *One of the things that the media have done with its sort of Watergate syndrome is that in their intensity to expose any official, public or university, for even trivial matters is that we're generating sort of a self-fulfilling prophecy. We say our leaders are all doing it, the next assumption is that everybody's doing it, and the third assumption is that everybody's expected to do it.*

And the resentment of the necessary but uneasy presence of the NCAA as absolver of crimes through the assignment of penitential acts is compounded by the fact that the private gestures of greed, vanity, and calculated temptation that lead to punishable infractions have truly public repercussions. This is seen not only in the damage done to an institution's reputation and often to its financial ability to support effectively all of its legitimate missions, but also in the altering of those fellowships that, as we have seen, are important and even critical:

> *So, you know what the NCAA does: take 'em off television. So you punish the little guy in the mountains or in the city who just wants to sit down and watch his team play. He didn't do anything wrong, and thousands of other fans who didn't do anything wrong can't watch either.*

Higher education has not been a prominent stage on which the great dramas of our democracy have been played out.   And the crisis in intercollegiate athletics may not bear serious comparison with those other dramas that now also hold our reluctant attention.   But for millions of Americans whose lives are intertwined in some way with college sports, this particular play has its own constrained fascination. The drama of "reform" cannot, of course, be performed through reconstituting a benign relationship between athletics and academe, because that was never present in the first place. In fact, forty years ago David Reisman speculated that college football (and we might now add, retroactively, college basketball) might eventually lose its importance as a game—as a subordinate though valuable counterpoint to the culture—and instead only reflect the qualities of the society into which it emerged through its obsessive emphasis on winning, its development of industrialized modes of operation, and a commercial sense of its own market value.[17] Nothing in the succeeding decades has altered the eminence of this possibility. As we have seen, the outward and visible form of intercollegiate sports is now more than ever shaped by commercial and technological emphases, and we seem to have avoided any concerted resistance to their continued separation in spirit and character from the university setting.

The messages that intercollegiate games are now sending back to us are troubling, deeply unsettling, in fact, if we can no longer regard our games as a reassuring juxtaposition of stability against the random nature of our ordinary existence. As briefly indicated already, the anxious signs are everywhere that their tarnished ethical character may indeed now reflect our values, that our college games are no different from other social citadels that have proved hollow. Such anxiety is reflected in the congressional action itself; in the allocation of funds by a private foundation for high-level investigations; in the public acknowledgment by the NCAA leadership of the need for reform; in weekly revelations of public dismay at cheating by coaches, athletes, and alumni or "boosters" at well known universities throughout the nation; in students and faculty rallying against covert actions by administrators or trustees who either compromise academic standards in favor of athletics or disdainfully isolate the athletic program from any semblance of presidential control. Within these signs of recognition and anxiety, however, the problematic question remains as to whether any genuine reform—any effective mode of controlling the illness—is possible, especially since that question must be posed against a century of rather gloomy evidence to the contrary.

Barbara Tuchman ended her essay, written in the midst of the most disconcerting domestic period in our recent history, not with an assertion of bleak discouragement, but with the observation that in human affairs the extrapolation of any trend is risky business: sooner or later a coping mechanism will emerge. The energy now being generated toward halting further separation between athletics and higher education, though not yet fully focused, nevertheless suggests that the beginning of a "coping mechanism" may be at hand. Certainly something of enormous value now seems widely perceived to be at issue, something in which we need to have faith. In our appraisal of this complex matter we have to recognize, indeed with some pride and gratitude, that our intercollegiate games are closely linked to the great rhythms of our democratic life in ways that the university is not. Even so, we should expect of them no less than from academe in the coherence and stability of their messages, and require that in the conduct of their affairs they exhibit that moderate honesty requisite to playing "within the rules." The latent vulnerability of college sports to a condition of infection and illness can only be lessened by strengthening and making more visible their bond with academe. The diagnosis and prescription contained in the following pages are offered as measures toward this end, as estimates of "what's good for the game" and, even more important, of "what's good for higher education."

NOTES

1. Probably the best treatment of the history of sport and its modern evolution may be found in Allen Guttmann, *From Ritual to Record: The Nature of Sports* (New York: Columbia University Press, 1978). See also Richard Mandell, *Sport: A Cultural History* (New York: Columbia University Press, 1984), esp. pp. 132-195, and "The Degradation of Sport," in Christopher Lasch, *The Culture of Narcissism* (New York: Norton, 1978), pp. 100-124.

2. While Dickens portrayed Americans as taking pride in their immunity from the claims of a tyrannical social system, *Martin Chuzzlewit* seems to illustrate his view that in the new country an unrecognized rigid social structure was actually being created by the pressure of public opinion and the unrestrained pursuit of financial gain. See also John Dizikes, "Charles Dickens, *Martin Chuzzlewit*, Mark Twain, and the Spirit of American Sports," in *Dickens Studies Annual 16* (New York: AMS Press, 1987), pp. 247-256.

3. Virginia Woolf, "American Fiction," reprinted in *"The Moment" and Other Essays* (London: Hogarth Press, 1952), pp. 101-104.

4. There is a wide and growing literature interpreting the "meanings" of sports within American culture, most of which consistently rejects Marxist and neo-Marxist claims that sport in Western society—through its ties to organized forms of

production (slightly suggested in the textual passage preceding this note) and its achievement-quantification orientation—ultimately is repressive of the human spirit. Among the most widely allusive and influential works are: Edwin Cady, *The Big Game: College Sports and American Life* (Knoxville: University of Tennessee Press, 1978); Allen Guttmann, *Sports Spectators* (New York: Columbia University Press, 1986); and A. Bartlett Giamatti, *Take Time for Paradise: Americans and Their Games* (New York: Summit Books, 1989). All are richly suggestive and cannot be reduced to neat summaries. However, each contains the pervasive themes that sports contests, perhaps especially the spectacular "big game," may be read as cultural texts in which the spectator-self, who witnesses in the game the individual player's attempt to create an integrity of purpose and movement (a kind of self-knowledge), is bound to other spectators in a sense of community as each strives for a comparable transformation, an imaginative re-creation of a freedom not ordinarily obtained—a sense of hope and possibility often also represented in the "American dream." See esp. Cady, pp. 92-93 and 225-232; Guttmann, pp. 176-85; and Giamatti, pp. 38-44, 103-105. That sports, especially intercollegiate games, create a significant sense of community and ideally possess certain possibilities for spiritual enhancement appear in other treatments of the subject; most recently, for example, in Donald Chu, *The Character of American Higher Education and Intercollegiate Sport* (Albany, NY: State University of New York Press, 1989), esp. pp. 155-182.

5. See John Underwood, "Student-Athletes: The Sham, the Shame," *Sports Illustrated* 52, no. 21 (May 19, 1980), pp. 36-72; Jerry Kirshenbaum, "An American Disgrace," ibid. 70, no. 9 (Feb. 27, 1989), pp. 16-34. Other parameters indicating the condition are easily found: for example, that offered by sportswriter Red Smith, "The Student Athlete," *New York Times* (Nov. 12, 1979), p. C-3; and George F. Will, who alludes to "the open sewer that runs through many campuses," "Let the NFL Pay for Its Farm Teams," *Washington Post* (Nov. 23, 1989), p. A-27. For a particularly strong statement of outrage at the alleged hypocrisy and seamy practices of college sports, see Rick Telander, *The Hundred Yard Lie: The Corruption of College Football and What We Can Do to Stop It* (New York: Simon & Schuster, 1989). The high level of public awareness of corruption in intercollegiate athletics may also be measured by the bold satire currently appearing in the sports comic strip "Tank McNamara": for example, in one column a coach sarcastically derogates the idea that "student-athletes" are seriously seeking an education; in another a coach cancels the scholarship of an "unproductive" runningback as a gesture to quiet public outrage at the multiple convictions for rape and assault charged against the school's football program; and in yet another the NCAA is denounced for hypocrisy and alleged self-interest in its stance on the drafting of underclassmen by the NFL.

6. This and all subsequent quotations in italics that do not have another attribution are taken from confidential interviews conducted by the authors with twenty-two current or recent university chief executive officers from all sections of the United States, representing all NCAA divisions; about two-thirds are CEOs at Division I-A institutions.

7. The financing of elaborate athletic physical plants apparently was strongly influenced by lay trustees from the business community who in the late nineteenth century began to be appointed to university governing boards and to determine

athletic policy. Ronald A. Smith, *Sports and Freedom: The Rise of Big-Time College Athletics* (New York: Oxford University Press, 1988), p. 98. On the matter of financing see also Guy Maxton Lewis, "The American Intercollegiate Football Spectacle, 1869-1917," (Ph.D. diss., University of Maryland, 1965), esp. chapters 4 and 5. The allusions to Yale football in the 1880s cited in this chapter are taken from Lewis.

8. Daniel J. Boorstin, *The Americans: The Democratic Experience* (New York: Random House, 1973), p. 148. Boorstin's allusion is to the "fellowships" formed by consumer habits.

9. Chu, already cited, notes that while there may be no substance to the myth that intercollegiate athletic competition improves the participant's moral or ethical character, the myth—like the one that athletics make money for the institution—lingers on in the mind of the public (p. 188). As to the nonathlete student population, a recent ad hoc-committee report from the University of North Carolina on the relationship between athletics and the university states that "students learn nothing from intercollegiate athletics that they could not learn from watching professional sports on television or attending analytical courses on sports." Quoted in the *Chronicle of Higher Education* 36 (February 7, 1990), p. B4.

10. For example, see reports of comments made by head football and basketball coaches and an athletic director at Division I-A institutions concerning committee recommendations for major program changes: one coach termed the committee "an unwarranted intrusion by professors into the athletic department," and the other said he "resents professors with expertise in other areas telling the athletic department what it should do." The athletic director at another university commented, "A major problem with the NCAA is that too many academicians who've never been in the trenches are making decisions they aren't qualified to make. I'm all for the presidents running their campuses, but they need to consult with their athletic people." Quoted in *NCAA News* (March 14, 1990), p. 3, and *Basketball Times* (February 15, 1989), p. 44.

11. Howard J. Savage et al., *American College Athletics* (New York: The Carnegie Foundation for the Advancement of Teaching, 1929). References and quotations are from the preface by Henry S. Pritchett, pp. xii-xv, xx-xxi, and from the text, p. 88.

12. F. Scott Fitzgerald, *The Great Gatsby*, in *Three Novels of F. Scott Fitzgerald*, ed. Malcolm Cowley (New York: Scribner's, 1953), pp. xx, 7.

13. David Riesman, *The Lonely Crowd* (New Haven: Yale University Press, 1950). Riesman would probably not agree wholly with this observation. Writing a year later in an article specifically addressing the development of football in America, he noted that the game then—with its growing specialization, two-platoon system, and developing workmanlike atmosphere—still could provide genuine personal satisfactions for players. Yet football had essentially become a cooperative enterprise where individual initiatives were potentially too costly "to the head coach, the budget, even the college itself" to be encouraged. Even then, the style of coaching was adapting itself accordingly to that we recognize today, as coaches saw their "need to be group-dynamics leaders rather than old-line straw bosses." David Riesman and Reuel Denny, "Football in America: A Study in Culture

Diffusion," *American Quarterly* 3 (Winter 1951), reprinted in *The Sporting Image: Readings in American Sport History*, ed. Paul J. Zingg (Lanham, MD: University Press of America, 1988), p. 221.

14. George H. Hanford, *An Inquiry into the Need for and Feasibility of a National Study of Intercollegiate Athletics; A Report to the American Council on Education* (Washington, DC: American Council on Education, 1974).

15. Barbara Tuchman, "History As Mirror," *The Atlantic* 232 (Sept. 1973), pp. 39-46. For a view comparable to that of Tuchman on "coping mechanisms," cited later in the text, see Robert Nisbet, *The Present Age: Progress and Anarchy in Modern America* (New York: Harper & Row, 1988), pp. 134-135.

16. Bill Moyers, *The Secret Government: The Constitution in Crisis*, first aired on public television November 4, 1987 (New York, WNET).

17. Riesman and Denny, "Football in America," p. 222.

Chapter *2*

Diagnosis: The Pathology of Infractions

SIGNS AND SYMPTOMS

Let me tell you this: every university president has to contend with the tendency of the institution to live a life comparable to that of the society it's a part of.

But the point is, it shouldn't be that way. I mean the university should always be the book by which we pull the standard up, not respond to it. What we've seen, for example, in this deteriorating relationship between athletics and the institution itself in terms of academic and behavioral standards is probably the most visible reflection of what has to be described as a serious ailment.

Unfortunately, our words such as "student-athlete" and "academics come first" sound hollow when we recognize what seems to be our economic value system—paying football coaches and athletic directors three or four times the salary of the president of the college and even four or five times that of the most senior and eminent member of the faculty. What we're doing is allowing the entertainment business and the professional ranks to be the model for our own activities on the campus; I think we're speaking out of both sides of our mouth.

These and uniformly similar observations by CEOs of many universities whose teams in football and basketball have had their full share of national prominence reflect a pervasive unease at the abortive condition whereby the subculture of intercollegiate athletics has become, in too many instances, essentially separated from the body of the host institution that gave it life. Inherent in these comments also is a perception of the complexity of the matter, an awareness that multiple social forces are somehow involved, and a sense that the frequent and widely publicized abuses in intercollegiate athletics constitute an ailing condition with grave, albeit subtle, long-range implications that have not yet been fully diagnosed, and therefore not effectively controlled.

As already discussed, college sports form the most arresting and spectacular play in our cultural theater and their dramatic appeal seems only likely to increase. But this powerful and celebratory display of intense competition belies the presence of recurring symptoms of a less vigorous condition. A simple statistical history of such symptoms, the public penalties imposed on NCAA member institutions for violations of regulations adopted by the membership itself, starkly reveals the extent, persistence, and severity of this condition, not one comparable to terminal cancer, to be sure, but nevertheless a persistent and lingering malady that continues to erode the association's ideals of equity, fair play, and amateurism in college sports.

During the period from October 1952 to October 1983, the NCAA infractions committee (or council) considered 1,334 cases, 272 of which resulted in public reprimand, censure or probation.[1] However, private reprimands were issued in an additional 573 cases in which there were minor, mostly technical and often inadvertent, violations judged not of sufficient importance to warrant public reprimand. The increasing sensitivity of the NCAA membership to the frequency of these overt transgressions and inadequate attention to administrative control is indicated by periodic increases in the severity of imposed penalties. Concern in the early 1980s reached a climax at the special convention in June 1985, when legislation was adopted to specify violations as "secondary" and "major," with minimum penalties established for the latter, including the so-called "death penalty." At this time also, legislation was revised to place greater emphasis on institutional control, assigning to the CEO explicit responsibility for the budget and audit of all athletic funds; for the review of a coach's outside compensation; and, in Division I, for the reporting of academic data on student-athletes. Even so, from 1983 through 1988, there was no statistical reduction in flagrant violations. The additional cases during this period in which public penalties were imposed, including sanctions which prevented postseason competition or television appearances, might suggest a higher frequency of violation, but no definite conclusion can be drawn from these data because factors such as the increased number of NCAA enforcement staff undoubtedly have affected this number.

Between 1952 and 1988, NCAA active institutional membership increased from 397 to 800. Of the 361 cases over this thirty-six-year period in which some form of public penalty was imposed, approximately 85 percent involved some type of violation in the recruitment of prospective student-athletes, usually the offering of financial inducements; and, as might be expected, most of the cases have involved the two principal "revenue" sports, football and basketball. Academic improprieties have been less frequent, but cases of admissions fraud, such as the submission on behalf of prospective student-athletes of modified transcripts or unearned high-school or junior-college credits, have been continually disclosed. Any realistic analysis, however, of the history of academic abuses would have to recognize that in 1973 the NCAA itself reduced the freshman eligibility requirement for student-athletes to a significantly lower level. "We ran out on standards in 1973," as one CEO puts it, "and we have never found our way back!"

Freshman eligibility had few academic conditions for the period between 1973 and 1986, the effective date of the "initial qualifier" legislation enacted as Proposition 48 in 1983. A relationship between the minimal requirements during this period and the relative infrequency of overt academic violations, even while recruitment violations were increasing, can be posited but not proven. Clearly it was not necessary during these years to use improper means to secure the admission of marginally prepared prospects: their admission was essentially unregulated in the first place. Yet even so, seven institutions—some with strong regional academic reputations—were placed on public probation in the years 1980-1982 for attempting just this type of academic fraud.

Although abuses appear to be more common and serious among institutions in Division I, because of their visibility, violations do in fact occur in Divisions II and III, where the opportunity for corruption, especially in Division III, may be enhanced because of relative neglect by NCAA enforcement attention.[2] Indeed, violations appear to be more common than is generally recognized.

> *It makes my blood run cold when people talk about Division III being the last bastion of athletic purity. The Division is large and complex; at some schools, on Saturday afternoon, people come out and sit on the lawn and you have a football game. And then you have other Division III schools with twelve coaches, not all on the payroll, but on the sidelines. Before this season, I was at a conference gathering and chatting with some coaches, and I said to one coach, "How are you going to do this year?" And he said, "Oh fine, we only lost a couple of kids and have all our redshirt freshmen." And I said, "Redshirt freshmen?" And he said, "Yeah, if you come to our college, we're now kind of a second-chance school, so everybody's going to play five years."*

I think we're at risk, if we aren't very, very careful, of Division III getting into Division I problems. One of the biggest mistakes a Division III president can make is not being careful about monitoring these athletic things. We tend to say, well it doesn't matter, the stakes are so small, we don't make any money at football. But cheating always matters.

The frequency of violations in Division III institutions was confirmed by more than one CEO, several athletic directors, and a former dean of a private liberal arts college in Division III. An athletic director commented as follows: "As you know, if you pick up a prospective student-athlete at the airport, that's one of his authorized 'paid visits' and you're supposed to be sure he knows that. But many schools never mention it; they pick him up and say, 'The coach can do it because he lives only five miles from the airport.' Division III schools just think they are so small, it won't matter, that it isn't really going to make a difference as to whether they get the student or not."

The former dean stated, "When I was dean of the college at _____, I learned that wealthy alumni thought nothing of providing room and board at a local hotel or in their own homes for outstanding tennis, golf, or lacrosse prospects during their campus visits. It goes on all the time. . . . In some instances a student-athlete would even be provided a room for the entire year, at no cost, in the home of an alumnus."

A superficial summary of the scope and general nature of the manifestations of an illness must, of course, fall far short of providing an accurate insight into the gravity of the ailment in specific cases or an understanding of the potential harm for what might be called the "population at risk"—those already exposed or even infected but still asymptomatic. However, a detailed review of two specific recent cases can help provide that discernment.

CASE A. In the spring of 1987, a prestigious university in Division I-A recruited and admitted a junior-college transfer student who had sufficient hours of transferable credit for admission but, as the faculty athletics representative subsequently determined, the number of hours was insufficient to establish eligibility. The athletic recruiting coordinator received this information after closing dates for enrolling the prospect either in summer-session courses at the university or at a community college. Still, the coordinator arranged a fraudulent enrollment in a community college from which the prospect received unearned academic credits that made him eligible for competition during the 1987 football season at the university. The credits were arranged and provided by a representative of the university's athletic interests who was an instructor in the community college district. The prospect did not pay any enrollment fees for the courses, and neither attended classes nor completed any academic work. In late August and early September 1987, the recruiting coordinator, who had transported the prospect to the community college to secure the counterfeit transcript, attempted to prevent university authorities from learning of the ineligibility of the student-athlete by instructing the young man and another student-athlete to provide false information.

CASE B. In 1988, following an extensive institutional investigation, a university admitted or accepted responsibility for nearly all of the more than forty violations found by the NCAA Infractions Committee. These violations primarily involved former members of the university's assistant football-coaching staff, a former athletic-department academic counselor and at least fourteen representatives of the institution's athletic interests, one of whom was a former member of the university's Board of Regents. Violations included: (1) promises of large sums of money (e.g., a $5,000 cash payment if the prospect would sign a National Letter of Intent to attend the university, a Nissan 300ZX automobile upon enrollment, and a $200 monthly allowance during the young man's attendance); (2) the provision of $5,000 to another prospect, delivered to his home after the young man signed a National Letter of Intent earlier that day; (3) arrangement for a third student-athlete to receive an automobile provided at no cost by representatives of the university's athletic interest; (4) a monthly cash allowance ranging from $50 to $200 for yet another student-athlete over a period of about twenty months, provided or arranged by a former assistant football coach and representative of the university's athletic interests; (5) certification of eligibility for a student-athlete to compete in three football games in 1984 when there was no official transcript on file for a course allegedly taken under a coach at another NCAA member institution with the intent to use the course to meet the NCAA satisfactory-progress requirements; (6) the encouragement to a prospect by former university assistant coaches to provide false information during interviews with an NCAA investigator; and (7) the involvement of a former assistant coach who secured the enrollment of a highly visible prospect and arranged for such benefits as $5,000 cash upon signing the National Letter of Intent, multiple cash gifts averaging $125 during the first year of enrollment and $200 during the second year, and an expensive sports car at no cost to the young man, with the title being placed in the name of the young man's brother and with all payments for the car and for insurance being made by three representatives of the university's athletic interests.

Each of these cases presents a wretched and depressing condition: grossly unethical behavior by athletic officials who knowingly violated the very institutional and NCAA regulations with which they had, in writing, certified their compliance; zealous, peculiarly inane attempts by "friends" of the institution to provide money and goods as modes of seduction; and, undoubtedly in the latter case, either cooperation or benign neglect by academic staff members charged to supervise admission and eligibility processes. In Case B, this attempt to subvert the institution's educational mission seems even more disheartening in that the university involved had been placed on probation with sanctions twice in the preceding eleven years for serious violations, and the football coach had also been cited previously for unethical conduct by the NCAA infractions committee. Further, as a result of these findings three additional institutions that had entered a bidding war for the athlete's services were also assigned NCAA penalties. Thus, in this case, the illness was not limited to this institution but spread outward to affect others.

Obviously many institutions have found ways to prevent serious impairment, even though they exist in an environment, such as that in Case B, where contact with the causes of illness are inevitable and may even result in incipient infections. Twenty-seven of the 105 institutions classified in Division I-A in 1988-1989 had at that time received no penalty (not even a public reprimand or censure) since the NCAA enforcement program was initiated in 1952. Sixteen of these have been ranked at least once in the Associated Press top twenty football teams in the period 1955-1988. (Only ten teams were ranked for the years 1962-1967.) The fact that two of these have been ranked twenty-two and twenty-one years, respectively, during this period is striking evidence that it is not necessary to cheat in order to win.

However, a disconcerting number of other institutions have not found ways to avoid impairment, despite the fact that NCAA enforcement policies provide that prior violations shall affect the severity of subsequent penalties. Figure 2.1 is a graphic presentation of the number of institutions in Division I-A, as of 1988-1989, under an NCAA penalty (including public reprimand, censure, or probation with various sanctions for one or more sports) during all or part of each academic year since 1952-1953 through 1988-1989. What is immediately most noticeable is the fact that the number of institutions under penalty has increased during the past decade, when 54 of the 105 Division I-A institutions were under penalty at least once. The mean number of institutions under penalty each year of the past decade was 16.4, compared with a mean of 9.5 for the preceding decade. A number of dynamic forces have contributed to this, such as the increase in number of enforcement staff members of the NCAA; and some of these will perhaps in time serve to help reduce the number and frequency of recurrence of violations. Nevertheless, there is cause for alarm in the fact that slightly less than one-third of the

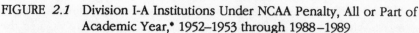

FIGURE *2.1* Division I-A Institutions Under NCAA Penalty, All or Part of Academic Year,* 1952–1953 through 1988–1989

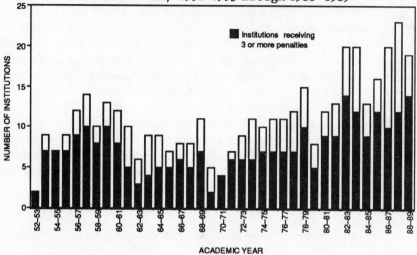

*Academic Year = August–May

institutions (thirty-three), each of which had three or more penalties, accounted for approximately two-thirds of the total academic years of penalties shown in this graph.

The increasing tendency of the NCAA membership to impose more severe penalties for major violations is illustrated in figure 2.2. It remains to be seen whether the more severe penalties adopted in 1985 will have a significant deterrent effect.

Within the multiple array of colleges and universities from throughout the country represented in these statistics, each undoubtedly with its own institutional personality and distinction, there would seem to be nevertheless some common pattern of relationships that has linked them together in acts of capitulation to potentially infectious causes that their own educational purposes and ethical commitments should have led them to confront and reject. What *is* the pattern? What *is* the link? What connects an institution publicly identified for the first time as committing an infraction with those institutions guilty of repeat violations whose revelations of payoffs and corruption seem to startle even the most supportive media and public? And what links all of these, as well as some Division II and III schools—which rationalize their cheating as insignificant—with the one "death penalty" institution where over a period of several years coaches, players, athletic and academic officials, trustees, and even state politicians gradually became imprisoned by their own acts of duplicity, arrogance, greed and fear?[3]

FIGURE *2.2* Duration of NCAA Penalties Imposed on Division I-A Institutions During Decades of 1950s through 1980s (through 1988–1989)

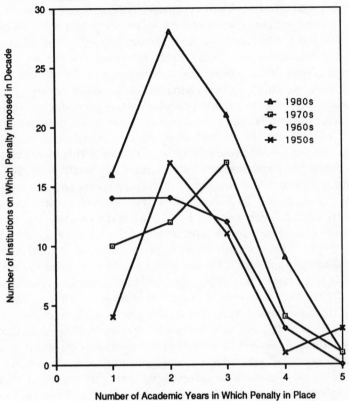

CAUSES: FUNDAMENTAL AND CONTRIBUTING

> *. . . we are all diseased*
> *And with our surfeiting and wanton hours*
> *Have brought ourselves into a burning fever,*
> *And we must bleed for it.*

This diagnosis by the Archbishop of York in Shakespeare's *Henry IV, Part 2* is set here as a deliberate intrusion to depersonalize for a moment the potentially volatile questions just raised. And yet this view of the infected condition of the body politic in fifteenth-century England, with its emphasis on the need for therapeutic measures of control, is not without some analogous relevance. The disease of civil strife—"of which," as the archbishop goes on to reflect, "our late King Richard, being infected, died"—has festered into a pervasive condition, stimulated by the confluence of such human actions as self-indulgence, intemperateness, ambition, abuse of power, and political betrayal. The lines imply that, in fact, the condition has always existed in a latent form, with the corpus of the state awaiting, as it were, an overt act of seditious force, which in this instance Henry himself had committed, for it to erupt and contaminate. Tudor historians often saw the great political rivalries and wars of the previous century in terms of disease and infection.

Interpreting cultural phenomena in terms of our own physical and emotional experience is an almost primitive and yet powerful way of thinking we are reluctant to relinquish. Shakespeare's metaphor, with its suggestive network of causative levels and latent illness, might serve as a literary harbinger of the modern scientific view of disease. This view can lead us further toward a dispassionate and yet revealing analysis of the vexing relationship between the subculture of college sports and the body of its university host. In fact, as Robert Nisbet has observed, medical metaphors, especially those "of sickness and health, applied to society, are doubtless responsible for as much redemptive action as the labels of good and evil."[4]

Since the 1950s, our understanding of the causes of physical disease has been enormously enhanced by the research and writing of the American microbiologist, Rene Dubos. Moving beyond the traditional scientific doctrine of specific etiology whereby laboratory experiments had long since demonstrated that disease states could be readily produced by introducing a single factor such as a virulent microorganism into a healthy animal, Dubos emphasized that a complete account of the causation of disease in any given case could rarely be reduced to the single-factor theory. Rather, he wrote, based on his own research on tuberculosis and other microbial infections, several determinants usually play a part in the causation of disease: a simple example is the benign but recurrent lesion of the fever blister, caused by the herpes virus—which is itself contracted by many people early in life and persists permanently somewhere in the tissues in a latent form until some provoking stimulus causes the infection to be manifest in the form of blisters. The stimulus transforming infection into disease may be a fever of unrelated origin, certain types of surgery, improper food, or excessive irradiation; but the herpes virus itself is merely the agent of infection, the instigator being an unrelated disturbance of the host. There are, in fact, both "fundamental" and "contributing" causes of disease.[5] In our attempts to understand the problems of intercollegiate athletics, it would appear that we continue to confuse the symptoms and causes of the disease. Consequently much of our corrective effort is directed toward the symptoms, rather than the fundamental causes. This is analogous to universal experience in the treatment of human ailments, where there is the related problem of relying on increase in medicine dosage to effect recovery:

When you're treating an ill patient increasing the size of the dose of medicine without understanding the fundamental causes is foolish. With abuses in athletics, I think we've often been content just to increase the dosage.

There is, of course, latent in any democratic institution, the Congress for example, the potential for an eruption of behavior alien to that institution's essential purpose. Because of the public visibility and protean capability of such institutions, however, we seldom recognize their constant susceptibility to the idle virus always awaiting an instigative force. Universities themselves, our "secular cathedrals" as they have been called, are certainly no more immune to corruption than government and business from behavioral patterns that seem analogous to those resulting in widely publicized scandals in those other institutions. Unethical and corrupting acts, the intentional publication of fraudulent data by a faculty member or research group, for example, surely occur from time to time. But these relatively rare incidents usually are not of a mercantile nature; rather, they are often ironic and counterproductive attempts to enhance the academic reputation of the institution, or of an individual or group, through a conscious manipulation of the interior processes of research and discovery central to the institution's very reason for existence.[6] Athletic abuses, however, are of a different order. Almost inevitably they move, as it were, outward from the university body, bringing college sports closer to assuming a microcosmic identity with the larger social order itself, a tendency which the presidential voices at the beginning of this chapter warned against.

We have already seen how the problems in college sports currently receiving so much attention and provoking so much moral outrage are really not significantly different in their nature from those that have occurred over the past century. Also, in an earlier section, we have noted the sense of dislocation that has characterized the historical relationship between the subculture of intercollegiate athletics and the larger environmental culture of the university to which it was originally attached. Now, however, the continuing frequency and intensity of those abuses, together with their sometimes brutal and inevitably deceitful guises, suggest that in far too many instances this sense of dislocation is almost complete. College sports, in fact, seem at times to have lost touch with their own story, their own history. And though we continue to view abuses as the result of such elements as the commercialism of intercollegiate athletics, the university sense of compulsion to provide entertainment for the public, and the professionalism of sports, these are but *contributing* or *secondary* causes. The *fundamental* causes are rejection or erosion of the educational mission of the university and the disregard for basic ethical values of behavior by those who administer, coach, play, or attach themselves to the environment in which these games are played.

To some extent this loss of memory may be related to the larger sense of separation from our social and ethical origins and from the common substructure of beliefs and understandings that determine the nature of our "cultural literacy." This concept finds expression, for example, in the American Council on Education's *Memorandum to the 41st President of the United States,* in which abuses in college sports are identified as one of the pervasive and highly visible "troubling developments" signifying that the social order may well "have lost touch with fundamental values and standards of ethical behavior."[7] Such signs may indeed be relevant to those who will write the history of our nation's economic and industrial decline in the last three decades. The connection between that decline and the well-documented retreat from academic standards in higher education that began in the 1960s seems inescapable; and, as we shall see presently, the relaxation in the 1970s of admission standards for college athletes is but a subset of that larger pattern:

> *Since about 1965–1966, we've let academic standards deteriorate to an absolutely appalling level. And at the same time we began to see this happen, we saw a deterioration of productivity standards in the workplace. And during this time frame in which we also helped to create this crisis in intercollegiate sports, we've also gone from the richest nation on earth to the largest debtor nation.[8]*

The many cases of cheating in athletics that persisted throughout the 1980s may indeed be relevant as social signifier, representing a kind of late and sad harvest along a continuum initiated by the social forces that contributed to the academic permissiveness and student protests of the Vietnam decade. But the point to be made here is that college sports are essentially a culture not sufficiently responsive to the educational and ethical rhythms of their environment and, left to their own dynamic, tend to seek constantly a life of their own outside that setting. Yet they must live there, within the university, and their consonant opposition to the resident value system is frustrating, sometimes hostile and defiant, but more often than not, strangely unconscious: that is, suffering a memory loss, not even recognizing their own alien presence. There is, in fact, considerable evidence to indicate that new members of the athletic community are quickly assimilated into a kind of "occupational" mode whereby they accept a certain deviance in their ethical behavior as an often necessary means for achieving organizational goals and objectives: the winning of intercollegiate athletic contests.[9]

How else can the actions in the two cases summarized above be explained? Whether incredibly amoral or consciously devious, these actions clearly subordinated the university's central mission of education to the calculated goal of increasing the football team's chances of winning. Each case also illustrates the characteristic condition whereby an infraction contributes to an infected environment, especially the second one with its network of participants: athletic department personnel, representatives of the institution's athletic interests, student-athletes together with their relatives and friends, and the responsible officials who permitted the student to compete when no transcript of the credit ostensibly, but in fact fraudulently, "earned" had been recorded. The very existence of such an isolated infection implies a more specific alienation from the very institution in whose name the games were played when one notes that:

- Before the beginning of each academic year student-athletes must sign, as a condition of eligibility for competition, a statement affirming that they are not in violation of the basic NCAA regulations on recruitment and extra benefit.
- Each athletic department member, excluding clerical staff, must annually sign an affidavit affirming that the individual has reported any knowledge of violations of NCAA legislation involving the institution.
- The CEO must formally attest, as a condition of eligibility for NCAA championships, that this process has been completed and that the institution is in compliance with all NCAA regulations.

In both Cases A and B, all signatures had been duly obtained.

But if the diagnosis of an infraction must first involve our recognition of its fundamental cause, the rejection by a separated subculture of the intellectual and humane values resident in the institutional host that contains it, we should recognize also that this sense of dislocation, of separation, has not been entirely self-imposed. As the application of Dubos's research illustrates, the possibility for an illness (infraction) is always present. The following expressions of frustration and judgment sounded by university presidents reaffirm those of Shakespeare's archbishop that we "have brought ourselves" into the condition of risk:

When I'm asked to speak to fraternity groups I tell them that if their organizations don't serve the academic purposes of the university, they might as well be sponsored by the local filling stations. Everything the university sponsors ought to be involved with the education of students, with learning—the learning that will shape their careers and the kind of lives they will lead. Now athletics can gain new friends for you, keep the alumni coming and all that—be great entertainment, but unless they contribute to this kind of learning, to our central mission, their games shouldn't be sponsored by the University of _____.

> *Don't give me all that stuff about character building, about opportunity for education. Only a small percentage of athletes in many of our football and basketball programs are graduating! Sure —athletics help to bring the campus community together, that sort of thing; but the only thing that validates their presence is the learning experiences the student receives. And if that's not happening, we've just failed, and we lack credibility with the public.*

> *I think that we just basically are saying that there's one thing in America important enough to set up separate rules for—the only thing important enough to society to really exempt you from many of the requirements of the university, and that's athletics. And don't think that our students don't see this. They accept it, don't challenge it, and carry that perception away with them into later life.*

"Illness," of course, is a term that may signify conditions as widely separated as the common cold and cancer. And it is easy to overemphasize and uniformly assign what may be an unwarranted dramatic quality to the relationship between athletics and higher education, overlooking the apparent condition of health in many intercollegiate programs. Here the risk of infection remains latent, for sport has not forgotten its history, and reinforces through its games many of the positive values of the collegiate scene, integrating the lives of student athletes into the academic goals of the institution. But in far too many other institutions the risk is enormously greater, particularly in those large state-supported ones more continually in the public eye, where the very multiplicity and decentralized scale of activity render intercollegiate sports less organic to the personal lives of students. Here the fissure between the educational mission and that of an athletic counterculture often becomes wide and visible, seen and cynically accepted by students and an indifferent public alike. Within that fissure, as we shall see, the hidden virus lies less well contained, more susceptible to excitation by one or more of the contributing causes which that counterculture continually engages. And, once more, the eruption of an infraction from the latent infectious state, the act of violation itself—whether it be the result of greed, egocentricity, calculated self-protection, an exchange of money or goods, or the arrangement for a prospect to cheat on his admissions test—exhibits a disastrous loss of memory. For what has been forgotten in these acts of ethical violation is that life within the body of the university, which in the midst of a rich diversity of idea and style nevertheless beats quietly, emphasizing each day in hundreds of classrooms and laboratories the ideals of intellectual honesty and integrity central to its mission of teaching and learning. And what displaces this quiet matrix of permanence and diversity is a life attuned to another rhythm, a life incessantly documented in the florid prose of the local press: relentless in its annual intensity of practice, conditioning, training, and peculiarly innocent in its ruthless discipline to a goal recorded only in the transient pattern of flashing scoreboard numerals at the end of a dozen autumn afternoons or two dozen winter nights.

That numerical pattern, of course, in the larger life of the university survives the darkened scoreboard for a brief period, reappearing in the next edition of the student newspaper, for example. But after the postgame hours of celebration or mourning, the numbers are gradually subsumed in the Sunday afternoon realities of preparing for the Monday morning chemistry exam, completing the paper on "Young Goodman Brown," or finishing the design project for Civil Engineering 401. And, while the score and game are being left behind on the one hand, as the attention of the university itself turns inward, they are being sustained outside the institution in a variety of ways: beginning with the Sunday afternoon replay of the game from a commercial television station, moving through the release on Monday night of rearrangements in team rankings by the national polls; and, for at least two days, enduring further analysis in the local, state, and perhaps even in the national media from every conceivable angle and statistic. By the middle of the week or so, while the chemistry exams are being returned and students are wishing they had looked more closely at Hawthorne's dark New England forest, an enormously complex array of economic interests are concentrating on the next game and a new cycle: film crews, television analysts, food vendors, motel staff, and, of course, sports reporters who declare that both coaches (not the student-players, but the coaches) "will be under tremendous pressure this week" no matter whether their teams won or lost the week before.

All in all, as we have seen in an earlier section, the spectacle of a major college football game is now firmly fixed as a unique form of cultural holiday in America. At the same time, however, that such happenings powerfully create images of nostalgic recollection and social identity for thousands of spectators, they also reinforce the tendency of college sports to forget its educational connections and to assume a separatist, at times almost commercial character. In a university of fifteen thousand undergraduates, the football team itself consists of only one hundred or so players, less than 1 percent of the student body. But in even moderately successful programs the team may play before forty or fifty thousand persons, only about one-fourth of whom are students. This population of one hundred student-athletes would normally be attended and coached by a staff whose size exceeds that of many of the university's academic departments.

What you often have is more assistant football coaches recruiting thirty football players a year than you have admissions officers recruiting an entire student body. . . . This disproportion is a very, very serious matter because the money and the opulence in the athletic program disconnects it from the rest of the university. . . . Cheating, outright corruption, maybe drugs and gambling—these are of course the worst abuses and everyone agrees with that. But these subtle abuses of disproportion are insidious. I mean when a department can hardly get up enough money to send a faculty member to a regional meeting to give a research paper and the team is traveling in splendor, or when most of our students are living like you and I lived—and how thousands of our alumni lived when they were here—and you see athletic dorms with year-round training tables of elaborate meals and piped-in stereo music, I tell you these are real concerns that usually aren't disclosed and they first cost you faculty support, but students are not far behind in noticing this division too.

Even in the best run universities, there are always serious deferred maintenance problems in classrooms and laboratories, but not in the athletic plant of those programs with big revenues. The programs, that is, that are clean, wouldn't think of cheating. But they say, "We've got to be competitive in our weight room and the concourse to the stadium and everything else," so they spend a lot of money to make the athletic plant magnificent. There's nothing wrong with this, but by comparison you've got a faculty group doing vital medical research in little cubby holes carved out of hallways; still, you've got a great weight room. I understand now the big thing is how many square feet your weight room has.

These observations of the physical separation on many campuses, especially those in NCAA Division I that conduct elaborate programs in the "revenue" sports of football and basketball, of the athletic subculture from the indigenous patterns of university life actually describe the symbolic sign of a more fundamental separation. For in this environment these sports find much of their rationale not within the university's educational mission but in their entertainment value. Entertainment of certain kinds, of course, has always been a part of the higher-education commitment, but only as an ancillary component of the curriculum. This has been especially true of the fine arts. Here student participation, often together with faculty members, in performing for an audience in a drama or musical ensemble, for example, where the dramatic or musical repertoire is typically selected to provide instructional diversity, is directly related to the student's disciplinary major—becoming a professional musician or actor-director. Or it is an activity the student chooses simply as an element of pleasurable experience, whether course credits toward graduation are earned or not.

This concept of entertainment that is student-centered and educational in its motivation prevails, at least conceptually, as a principle in the operation of intercollegiate athletic programs of Division III institutions. In seeking to integrate the objectives of athletic competition with the academic and developmental experience of the student and "to assure the integration of athletes with other students . . . the college places special importance on the impact of athletics on the participants rather than on spectators." In these programs, as the division statement of philosophy continues, it is the institutional internal community that is addressed rather than "the general public and its entertainment needs."[10]

Here the ideal of college sports assuming their proper and, perhaps, only logical justification through an "internal" orientation is defined in part through a rejection of their relationship to the "entertainment needs" of society. The phrase is indeed illuminating and in its honest and conservative assessment of the scope and purposes of one level of athletic competition in America, it invites comparison with the realistic assessment on the part of Division I institutions. In its statement of athletic philosophy, the word "entertainment" is not used, but that division frankly emphasizes the "regional and national" scope of its athletic programs, its recruitment of student-athletes, and its member sponsorship "at the highest feasible level" of one or both of the traditional spectator-oriented, income-producing sports of football and basketball. Competition at this order of magnitude clearly assumes a commitment to entertain a general public far removed from the state or territorial dominions of a given institution.

There is, of course, nothing particularly logical about the commitment to entertain both a local and national audience through college sports. Although members of a Division I institutional basketball team may earn a few credits toward graduation in the area of physical education by enrolling in a course called "Varsity Basketball," the activity of intercollegiate competition in the game of basketball will not, as implied above, bear an academic analogy with other undergraduate modes of public performance that are firmly rooted in the curriculum and major field of the student.[11] Nor can one find persuasive such attempts to justify a higher-education "obligation" to provide mass entertainment through sports as that offered by James Michener, who sees such an obligation as directly analogous to that of university extension agents delivering to the public research results developed by the institution.[12] There is, however, small merit in attempting to justify logically and intellectually a presence both intransigent and mercurial, a presence that exists in direct response to what Michener accurately identifies as the unique "demand" by Americans that its universities provide this particular form of public festivity.

This demand-acceptance pattern, evolving as it has since the turn of the century, forms a kind of minor illustrative history of the democratic symbiosis between public desires and the willingness, however reluctant, of higher education to accommodate them. Of course, higher education itself has often been successful in utilizing the undeniable appeal and entertainment power of sports to strengthen its ties with many constituencies and to affect either directly or indirectly its base of financial support. It is widely believed that athletic visibility may increase the opportunities for access to key decision makers for major institutional contributions; and it is much easier to attract state legislators to a reception or dinner during budget hearings if the coach of a winning basketball or football team is present—with legislators usually seeing more advantage to being photographed with the coach than with the university president. But to some extent this type of justification, economic and sociological rather than academic, tends to emphasize further the tenuous and separatist relationship that athletics in large-scale operations seem to have with the institution's central mission. In fact, accumulating evidence as well as the observations of university CEOs seems to support the view that athletic success stimulates private giving essentially for athletics but that there is no positive correlation between such success and contributions by alumni for academic programs.[13]

Many Division I athletic programs throughout the nation are able to keep in remarkable balance these separatist tendencies, the stresses of mass entertainment, the consonant pressure to secure the financial support necessary to sustain a magnificent array of facilities, and, certainly, the ethical stamina requisite for constant vigilance:

> *I ought to take time every night to bow down and give thanks for the integrity of the people I'm privileged to work with here. All the potential for scandal and these rock-solid people just bend over backward; I can tell you stories about all the ways they reduce risks. If you've had any experience at all in being responsible for a major athletic program, you can never sleep like a baby—as long as the enterprise is connected with all this money, is so attractive, and you've got thousands and thousands of people who are boosters, you've got all the potential for a disaster.*

Such accomplishments have much to do with winning records in one or both of the two major sports. However, other programs, as shown below, committed to the same competitive level and caught irrevocably by the demand for public entertainment, have not been so successful financially and have become thereby a population at risk, potentially much closer to that other group of programs that, as the continuing athletic scandals remind us, have indeed failed to keep the balance, capitulated to the pressures—commercial or otherwise—and suffered a disastrous loss of memory, forgetting in their zeal to achieve at "the highest feasible level" the essential criterion justifying their team's presence on the field.

> *It's frightening to recognize that these sports have become so financially a part of America that they have created the impression that a major role*

of a university is to entertain its alumni and supporters. And I mean that the demand is not just to entertain but to entertain at a certain level. And this tremendous fix the public has on sports leads to the pressure to recruit a 290-pound lineman who appears to have almost no chance of academic success at _____. That's where the trouble comes.

This presidential remark, expressing as it does the kind of personal and institutional stress inherent in the perilous act of balancing academic integrity, entertainment—"winning" entertainment—and the enormous costs associated with major college sports, finds a kind of cynical response in the opening couplet of a recent *New York Times* column entitled "Root of All Sport Is $$$$":

When that ol' devil auditor comes to mark against your name,
He marks not if you won or lost but how much you banked from fame.[14]

This witty but almost casual public affirmation that college athletics appear more commercial than collegial emphasizes also the interrelated tensions or matrix of contributing causes that may stimulate the inherent separatist tendencies of big-time sports and move a given program into a condition of illness. While many infractions, as we shall see presently, undoubtedly are caused by egocentric motives on the part of team "boosters," the pressure to win in order to achieve the "fame" and how much can be "banked" from it so that the costly athletic enterprise itself can be sustained is a stark economic reality each major program faces annually. It is not uncommon, for example, to see even a Division I institution transferring a "home" football game to a metropolitan or other site presumably advantageous to the opponent in order to secure a larger financial return. In such cases economic urgency brusquely displaces any social or entertainment values the game may bestow on students and local supporters.

The costs for any program are perplexing, and for some they are overwhelming. Data accumulated over the past two decades by the NCAA show that annual operating budgets for athletic programs have increased annually at a rate consistently exceeding that of inflation, a phenomenon that much resembles that of the health industry with its disproportionately escalating medical costs. The accompanying table gives some indication of the serious financial problems many institutions, at all NCAA levels, are encountering.

Pressure to win in order to secure sufficient financial returns from gate receipts and television appearances to meet the enormous costs of a large multisport program is one dimension of the problem, and it certainly may be a causative agent in the pathology of infractions. Albeit an extremely important causative agent, and one that must be addressed more effectively, commercialism is only a contributing cause, not a fundamental one. A number

TABLE *2.1*   Estimated Expenditures and Prevalence/Amounts of Deficits for
Athletic Programs in NCAA Member Institutions, FY 1988[15]

DIVISION	EXPENDITURES		PERCENT WITH DEFICIT	AVERAGE DEFICIT
	AVERAGE	MAXIMUM		
I-A	$9,000,000	$18,000,000	35	$1,000,000
I-AA	3,400,000	5,000,000	60	800,000
I-AAA*	1,500,000	2,500,000	70	600,000
II**	1,200,000	2,500,000	75	500,000
II*	800,000	1,000,000	70	300,000
III**	600,000	3,500,000	92	300,000
III*	300,000	1,000,000	70	125,000

*Without football
**With football

of reasons support this thesis. If "big money" were the "root cause of all problems in college sports," as many are affirming, one would expect more notorious violations of NCAA regulations in basketball during the past decade, prompted by the pressure to win and the pressure especially to reach the Division I men's Basketball Tournament in order to share in the striking escalation of teams' shares from that tournament during this period. Analysis of the tournament payoff and of NCAA penalties in which there were violations in basketball during the past two decades fails, however, to support such a relationship (see Figure 2.3). To be sure, the number of penalties for violations cannot be equated with frequency of cheating, but these data do have relevance, and they are the only objective measure available for testing such a hypothesis.

There is further evidence that however pervasive and insidious it is, commercialism is not a fundamental cause of abuses in college sports. Some schools with athletic expenditures in the upper range of all Division I-A institutions are among the leaders in rankings and won-loss records during the past thirty-five years. These same institutions have never had a public penalty in any sport. Finally, on this point, there is striking evidence of widespread abuses in Division III, where commercialism is certainly not the causative agent.

And what of those Division III programs in the 92 percent or 70 percent deficit category? With relatively low, perhaps mostly local, game attendance figures and with almost no chance at television or tournament-play-off revenue, their sports programs cannot possibly support themselves. But many schools in this division, especially private ones, derive their institutional operating budgets from two sources, endowment and student tuition, and there is evidence to indicate that sports at this level may assume a utilitarian form quite beyond the idealistic statement of division philosophies quoted above.

So you're trying to keep a private institution open and you need money. We don't get it at the gate—we charge two bucks or something like that so that families of three or four can spend ten dollars, have a hot dog, come to the games and have a good time. Kids get in free. We make five hundred a year or something, it's just nothing. But I'll tell you, success in these programs is noted, in the press for sure, and students way off see it and think "I might like that school."

This point was confirmed by an athletic director:

There's absolutely no question about it. Many Division III institutions are struggling to stay open. And in many of those cases, they're staying open with athletes. This is not the survival of an athletic program but of an institution. I know for a fact that coaches at some of these schools are told they've got to bring in twenty-five players a year. Now these are schools that don't have a large pool of applicants. They're really just trying to stay alive and believe that a winning team can get them the visibility and increase the headcount.

FIGURE *2.3*   NCAA Division I Men's Basketball: Tournament Team's Share, 1970–1989 and Penalties in Academic Years 1970–1971 through 1988–1989 for Which There Were Violations in Basketball

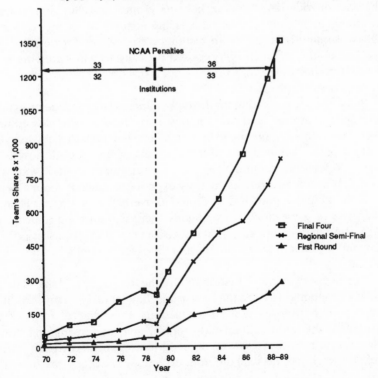

The visibility of an institution through success in athletics does serve to attract nonathlete students. Specifically, for example, in recent years schools winning the Division I basketball championship have noted significant increases in applications. And, at Division III level, athletic success, and the peril of cultivating that success, may be for some schools absolutely critical. As noted earlier, abuses in Division III are much more common than generally recognized.

Increased emphasis by athletic programs on aggressive commercial practices was inevitable in view of accelerating costs of operations and the inadequacy of such revenue sources as gate receipts, contributions from alumni, and allocations from student-activity fees. But, as we have seen already in presidential observations concerning palatial facilities, the uses to which such funds have often been put undoubtedly have contributed to the perception of intercollegiate athletics as a business separated from the institution's educational program. Not the least of these is the scale of what is called the "compensation package" for coaches in the major sports, especially highly successful ones in Divisions I-A and I-AAA. Institutional contributions to this compensation have generally been constrained because of comparisons with the salary of the chief executive officer, but the supplements from sports-related outside income have increased dramatically: for instance, contracts with manufacturers of athletic apparel (in return for which team members wear the company product), consulting fees, housing or annuities provided by alumni or "booster" groups, and television programs. Such arrangements have evoked increasing concern in recent years about conflicts of interest, or use of an institution's resources for personal gain, which contributes to much self-imposed pressure to win—pressure that is then transferred to the team.[16] (This matter is discussed further in the section titled "Finances" in chap. 4.)

Prospects are not strong for the type of increasing revenue growth that college sports have enjoyed over the past two decades. The blessed union between mass entertainment and high revenue sources, which the televising of college games seemed to confirm throughout this period, now is less certain. Television continues to exert great financial and "exposure" influence, but athletic directors are now expressing concern about a decline in football stadium attendance, attributed to overexposure on television and the vagaries of game time; consequently there is a growing reluctance to change game starting times on short notice for television purposes, as well as a comparable concern about late starting times for basketball games played in-season.

One of the most unfortunate results of the frequency and size of deficits in athletic programs has been the increasing elimination by many institutions of non-revenue sports. While such actions are a logical form of cost containment, the sports eliminated—tennis, golf, and swimming, for example—are those that are less team oriented, less regimented in character, and that often attract students with different experiential backgrounds from those participating in football and basketball. Thus the financial rationale may not only deprive "other" students from intercollegiate competition but may also reinforce the unfortunate isolationist identity that the so-called "major" sports seem to assume.

Despite the very real existence, however, in large university settings of a "two cultures" relationship involving educational mission and the athletic enterprise, operationally it is always the whole that is ultimately responsible for the part. NCAA regulations require a coach to report annually—to the CEO, through the athletic director—all athletically related income and benefits from sources outside the institution. They also prohibit the use, directly or by implication, of the institution's name or logo in the endorsement of commercial products without prior approval from the institution. Current practices suggest that the coach is more of a free agent in this regard than are faculty engaged in extramural consulting, but as one president observed, "If there's any criticism of this, or anything wrong with that source of compensation, the president has to answer for it." Likewise, in case of an alleged infraction the CEO and not the coach must be the leader of the institution's defense and negotiations with the NCAA.

Along with the coach and athletic director, the CEO is obviously the key figure in setting the tone of institutional control of the athletic program. The insidious pressures to win, which can often become a cause contributing to the eruption of an infraction, do not generally come from within the collegiate structure. As long as faculty and staff have confidence in the CEO's own integrity and emphasis on strong academic standards, they have shown little interest in becoming involved in matters of athletic governance.

The faculty may be a bit cynical and will put up with buying a kid a T-shirt or even a plane ticket, but they will not put up with changing transcripts or cheating on entrance exams.

Their attitude and that of the students too, when it's another school, "Well—we always knew those people were outlaws." But when it happens at their school, they're generally ashamed, embarrassed, like we all are—and that's the way it should be.

While a university president may fully understand the internal assurances of support for honest and forthright leadership in times of difficulty with administering the athletic program, he or she also recognizes that the peculiar nature of the structure and decentralized forms of decision making in higher education are often themselves relevant to the continuing recurrence of problems in college sports. At its best, a university is an organization of multiple purposes and modes of achieving them, organized around a loose confederacy of trust and understanding shared by faculty and administration in the quality and ethical nature of the institution's effort in the discovery, interpretation and transmission of knowledge. Though there is much autonomy in the way academic affairs are conducted by, say, some seventy-five departments organized within a dozen colleges in a public university of eighteen thousand students, they are yet linked in professional and intellectual ways. There is an economic linkage also, since all share in a budget dedicated from public or private funds to the teaching and research functions. There are no such linkages between academic and athletic departments. As we have seen already, higher education's response to public demand that college sports provide mass entertainment has contributed to their commercial disposition; and athletic departments, largely responsible for raising their budgets from noninstitutional sources, have developed great skill in forging alliances with strong political and economic constituencies.[17]

It would certainly be unfair to CEOs as a class to emphasize without qualification that a pervasive contributing cause to the spread of illness has been the failure of the front office to exert control of athletics when it has knowledge of local improprieties. Yet there are a number of recorded instances of such failure in infractions cases of the last several years. Most CEOs, of course, want their programs to be clean, while at the same time to make money, and project a favorable institutional image. And some, doubtless, would prefer for this difficult balancing act to be somehow maintained while they themselves attend to pressing academic or critical fund-raising matters and at the same time avoid the risk of placing such constraints on the athletic program that important constituencies with which it has formed close ties will be alienated from supporting the institution.

The presence of external groups, mostly alumni, and their potential power to affect the subordination of educational mission to athletic goals is nothing new. For example, long before the appearance of an effective national bureaucracy with assigned authority to control the sport of football, university faculty and administrators, alarmed over the game's growing brutality and, even then, its commercial dimensions, were generally opposed in their attempts at temperate legislation. The Carnegie Foundation for the Advancement of Teaching reported in 1911 that the University of Michigan, under the influence of the Chicago alumni club, had for years against faculty protests "tolerated a situation in athletics that was thoroughly demoralizing"; and in the same year the president of the University of Alabama, John W. Abercrombie, resigned in protest against alumni influence in athletic affairs, the issue of subsidized athletes, and the lack of proper academic standards in the sports program, stating that he would not "preside over a corruptly conducted athletic club" carrying the university name.[18]

The fervent sports loyalty of those wild and unregulated years still survives, of course, in many alumni hearts, and when carried to excessive levels, which are more often than not beyond the university's oblique form of control, it can contribute to the corruption of the very sports and institution it professes to cherish.

> *After I recommended that the coach be terminated for all that he had done, it got around that I just wasn't true-blue. One of our alumni asked me why I didn't abolish the biology department and use that money to help the football team. By God, I couldn't believe it. This was a really nice guy, supportive, and a responsible corporate figure, but on the subject of athletics, well. . . .*

Fortunately for most university presidents, the control of fervent external groups is a matter of keeping the larger university purposes and their need for financial support in some perspective. This must be balanced against the emotional and psychological response that such groups usually have toward athletics, and particularly, as already discussed, to the mysteriously nostalgic confluence of the football season and the beginning of a new academic year. Indeed, as one CEO observed, "most alums do keep it in perspective, even though it may be harder for them to get excited about a distinguished biologist than about a flashy quarterback." But this grateful presidential tribute must be qualified with other observations, almost desperate in their frustration, which essentially recognize that when this perspective disappears, when the memory fails, the latent disease can quickly emerge whether the contributing cause be a premeditated—or even foolish—gesture of unauthorized gifts to an athlete, thus corrupting the amateur status, or a sinister form of egocentricity:[19]

> *Don't do anything unless we ask you to. We recognize your support, we love you, but in your contact with student-athletes and coaches, don't do anything unless we ask you to.*

> *Sometimes you've just got to be very direct, and I've said to my AD, "If there's a booster who sort of likes to hang around and talk to the players and you're worried about him, introduce me because I've got something to say." And I tell him that he does not have enough money, if he gave it all to the university, to pay for the damage and embarrassment he would cause by committing an act that would get us into serious trouble.*

> *It's not just alumni, there's also this group around the program all the time who are wealthy and their lives seem to be so barren, empty, without meaning, and they try to get their kicks from being around a successful*

athletic program. They just love this identification with the coach and the players; there's a kind of reflected glow for them.

This latter observation especially suggests that the image of the hectic sports booster consumed only by a frenzied desire to see the team win is no more complete than those of the dumb jock or absentminded professor. The ambition to be an influential and recognized member of the power structure centered around a successful and highly visible athletic program is a motivating force that is ready and waiting to complete those external linkages described above, which semiautonomous athletic departments are constantly seeking.

You know, you hear frequently, "Well, we're not the problem, it's the alumni who've gone crazy." I really don't agree. I don't think alumni go crazy very often. I think what happens is the coaches stimulate this or that alumnus to do things they can't do themselves.

And, to be sure, within such an infected environment, booster ambition may find its counterpart in the egocentric drives of the figure who has the most to gain (and perhaps to lose) by the act of cheating. The widely perpetuated myth of a coach's job insecurity and its causal relationship to the anatomy of an infraction may have no more substance than that of the absence of infection and disease among Division III colleges with their "small-time" sports programs. We tend to think of behavior that leads to an infraction as cheap, tawdry, and depersonalized acts related only to public pressures to win and to job retention. But a coach is subject to the same flaws in the human condition as the booster. And his ethical sense may be obscured actually for comparable reasons.

In plain fact I think that in Division I-A most of the cheating is done by coaches who want to win for the security of their job only because the job provides most of the things their ego wants: money, influence, recognition, power—all those things. To say all these people have to cheat because they are pressured by the institution, the president, the AD, the fans or somebody—that's a cop-out. . . . A lot of them cheat because they want to win themselves no matter what else; they want what goes with winning. . . . The pressure is self-generated.[20]

And when this human network, whose form and strength take shape well beyond the institutional structure, is extended to the governing board itself, then the ability of the CEO is even further compromised in securing proper authority for control of athletics, even though he or she must ultimately answer for that responsibility—to the faculty and students, the public, and the NCAA.

This compromising of the university CEO's authority by the intrusion, either directly or indirectly, of the governing board into the decision-making process about athletics is one of the most lamentable ways in which the often imprecise governance structure of higher education becomes a contributing cause to abuses in athletics. Yet in the past decade a number of such cases have been documented and widely publicized. In one of these, the CEO resigned in the face of the governing board's refusal to support his efforts to correct abuses in the program. That case was an isolated instance only in its publicity.

> *In any honest treatment of this problem, the ultimate line of defense is integrity and vigilance by the board, the CEO, the AD, and the coaches; but if the governing board consists of people who are actually violating the rules or cozy with people who do, you're whipped before you start. There are eight or ten presidencies in my own memory, not just the two obvious ones, whose dismissals originated in the athletic thing.*

> *In the midst of all the turmoil I've been engaged in over athletics, I've found my board to be 100 percent supportive of integrity, but I do know from talking with my colleagues that my situation was more rare than it is common; and we all know good college presidents who, when they told their boards they were going to take action to clean up athletic problems, found themselves out of a job the same day.*

The occasional but not uncommon chorus of judgment, which at the very highest level of institutional governance may sacrifice presidential leadership to athletic interests, can also subordinate the university's central mission even further in a hostile response to proposed academic standards applicable to all students because of their presumed negative impact on the ability of inadequately prepared student-athletes to remain eligible.

> *In my own knowledge and experience relative to several institutions, I surely do know of specific instances where trustees have had such concern for the athletic program that they did not act rationally in evaluating academic proposals.*

Nowhere than in acts such as these is the health and integrity of the university body more at risk from the network of interrelated causes clustered around the athletic subculture. Fortunately, the great majority of colleges and universities apparently do not experience this type of potentially fatal intrusion.

> *Most of our trustees serve on major corporation boards and they understand their role, they're interested in broad policy matters. They want to know important things, of course, but they would be shocked, insulted, if I asked them to become involved in an athletic policy decision.*

Yet over the past twenty years an average of thirteen (12 percent) of the institutions in Division I-A received or continued under some form of NCAA penalty each year; documented evidence in many of these cases indicates that an influential coalition of athletic staff, external supporters, and governing board members has been an important contributing cause leading to the infraction itself. And, as indicated above, the silent, unreported compromises against institutional integrity made in the name of athletic interests, especially among Division III members, probably render the 12 percent figure quite modest as an indicator of the prevalence of abuses. One Division III CEO estimated that 25 percent of institutions at that level have in the past few years committed infractions that have gone unreported and undetected.

The athletic enterprise, with its separatist inclinations and its commercial-public entertainment dimensions, is undoubtedly a powerful influence on the predisposition of higher education, identified at the beginning of this chapter, to be less a model and critic than a mirror for the social order. Higher education itself in its own uncertain approaches to the governance of its athletic programs has certainly contributed to conditions wherein the assumed prerogatives of these programs have compromised educational mission. But in their attempts to communicate to the public the importance of quality education and the primacy it should have over the level of excellence in athletic performance, universities have been little assisted by the media.

Ironically, the one truly significant opportunity a university may have to bring a large audience into its classrooms or laboratories—to let that public really see the intellectual and scientific environment in which they have placed their daughters and sons—is the brief period at halftime of a televised athletic contest. The brevity of this encounter, which will not be endlessly re-run as are fragments of the game that the audience has already seen (and that hundreds of thousands will see yet again on the coach's talk show the next day) is only a visual parallel to comparable emphases in the print media. Every small-town newspaper, for example, has its sports editor and staff who daily report athletic goings-on at the local high school, the state and regional universities, even those in the professional realm.

Our university is obviously located in a very big metropolitan area, with another major institution and two colleges within the commuting area. At each of our basketball games, there'll be six or seven sportswriters. That's great; we like the coverage. But the largest newspaper around has only one —get this, one —writer assigned to cover educational matters for all of us —and the public schools too!

There are few if any complaints about this, of course. The media, including television, in its encompassing treatment of sports merely responds to what the public desires. And, partly as a result, the university itself remains in its purposes and modes of conduct the least understood of democratic institutions, its one visible and significant connection to the lives of most Americans being intercollegiate athletics. The influence of the media on our cultural assimilation of intercollegiate games and their social meanings has a long history. For example, important organizational reforms in the game of football itself were stimulated early in the century by the deaths and injuries resulting from football contests and by the remarkable conjunction of a newspaper photo in 1905 showing the battered body of a player emerging from the Swarthmore-Penn game coming to the outraged attention of Theodore Roosevelt, our first sports-minded president. And as popular culture began to receive increased photographic and written coverage, especially in the Hearst newspapers beginning about 1895, accounts of football games and the heroics of players with as many Irish, Polish, and Jewish names as Anglo-Saxon ones made clear to the nation that here was a game that was somehow democratic, one that had moved far beyond its elitist origins at such schools as Harvard and Yale.[21]

Sports reporting, however, in the printed media has remained primarily descriptive rather than analytical. To be sure, in the past decade, aggressive use of open-records laws has produced some notable exceptions in investigative reporting of improprieties in college sports, although much of this analysis has been written by reporters other than sports columnists. Editorial attitudes on this subject remain judgmental, perhaps even hypocritical in complaining loudly about such scandals while not recognizing, or admitting, that their own reporting emphases have contributed to the problem.

For example, the press in recent years has often assumed a contradictory position in reporting about academic standards for freshman athletic eligibility. While on the one hand, the absence of meaningful standards for a decade or so and the resulting exploitation of many student-athletes were properly deplored, on the other, universities and the NCAA have often been strongly criticized for adopting even minimal academic standards to help prevent such abuse. Clarification in the public press of such points as the difference between institutional standards for admission and those for athletic eligibility have been particularly scarce. Instead, charges of racism and social injustice have been frequent as these new standards, which in any rational appraisal emerge as hardly rigorous for most of the institutions to which they apply, are characterized to be particularly inhibiting to the potential eligibility of minority students.

> *I talked with a group of sportswriters on campus today, and I had a confrontation with one of them, who covers our sports all the time in a statewide paper, over his reporting about partial qualifiers. I asked why he had not explained what a partial qualifier was. At first, he stated that he had, but when challenged, he reviewed his material and said, "You're right, I haven't." I told him it appeared that when he wrote his stinging editorial rebuking us for trying to eliminate access, when no one in the world could ever show that we've tried to do that, he had gotten caught up in the way this was being made a racial issue in the national media.*

What has frustrated this university president essentially is the tendency of the media to reinforce the isolation of athletics from the university body. The dramatic arrival of the talented black athlete on the intercollegiate scene and his rapid assumption of a dominant presence in basketball and certainly a prominent one in football might be regarded as the third stage in the assimilation by American college sports of cultural and ethnic patterns.[22] That arrival, of course, coincided with the unsettling antiuniversity student protests of the late 1960s and early 1970s, which now, in retrospect, appear to have been animated as much by student opposition to academic discipline and to the competitiveness of intellectual achievement as by civil-rights issues and those inherent in the Vietnam war.[23]

It was within this larger context, infused by political and social pressures on universities to lower their admissions standards—pressures readily accommodated by some faculty administrators and also by the NCAA—that many institutions in an effort to achieve success in athletics, to "turn a program around," admitted large numbers of student-athletes who clearly were inadequately prepared for academic success. And it was during these years, from about 1970-1983, as abundant evidence substantiates, that these young people were institutionally guided in ways to permit them to maintain their eligibility without having made even minimal progress toward a degree.

> *When we as faculties discovered in the late 1960s—at least in our large public universities—that we didn't have to do all those things which weren't so pleasant, I think athletics were the most obvious casualty. We became increasingly persuaded that the undergraduate classroom just wasn't our primary responsibility. We abandoned it for something else.*

I know research and public service matter vitally. But as we embraced the tendency to take care of our own narrow corners, those poorly prepared student-athletes admitted then were just ignored academically.

It is against this complex social background that the discussion and initiation by the NCAA and its membership from 1983-1986 of higher academic standards for freshman and continuing athletic eligibility should be understood. In fact, these efforts cannot be accurately appraised without the perception that they are closely linked to the attempt by higher education to reconstruct and reclaim a curricular and academic coherence that in many institutions disappeared in the disarray of protest some twenty years ago. The concerns and commitments behind Proposition 48 are directly related to the current heated debates over "cultural illiteracy."

Admittedly, this is a difficult matter. But the media, including some editorial writers on prestigious newspapers and public figures from major television networks—abetted, of course, by some coaches whose statements have opposed the positions of their own institutions—have become an influential causative agent within the anatomy of latent infection and illness by implying on this one issue that educational principles be subordinated to athletic interests. These voices have argued with great force and considerable irony that compromises in the admission and academic eligibility of an athlete-student be made, the kind of compromises that would in fact be unthinkable in the competitive world of the practice field or court. Unfortunately, it has been too little noted that one of the genuine success stories in higher education has been the power of collegiate sports in assimilating successfully the principal social issue the nation has encountered since World War II.

Let me give you a sign of health. There probably isn't any other enterprise in American life, except possibly the entertainment industry, where the races have learned to work together and support each other mutually any better than in intercollegiate athletics.

If the university is our least understood institution, it is also our most egalitarian and socially idealistic. Its admirable emphasis in recent years on academic support services to increase the chances of success for poorly prepared student-athletes may be, indeed, partly motivated by a desire for prosperity in athletic programs. But it may be as well a self-conscious action for past, and continuing, exploitation of black athletes in particular. As the self-consciousness of the nation to compensate for past discrimination seems to be declining, there are many signs that higher education, even with its troubling awareness of athletics as "another culture," is gradually seeking ways to cultivate for its student-athletes a self-image of dignity and place.

That goal, however, is thwarted or at least compromised by the circumstances surrounding the student-athlete's recruitment and matriculation. Recruitment is now only slightly less intense than the playing out of the game schedule itself. Reporting from this front begins even before the ending of high-school football and basketball seasons and is stimulated in midwinter by local, regional and national analyses of who the top prospects are and their ratings by commercial sources and the media. Many prospects will receive fifty to one hundred institutional contacts even before the senior high-school season begins, and the stresses brought on student, family, high-school coach and principal are, as widely reported, of enormous magnitude.

When you've got many influential alumni, even legislators involved, you know you've got athletic budget problems, I mean —you can't imagine— it's just unbelievable pressure to get this kid in school.

The latest and, presumably, authoritative report from the field is that 25 percent of athletic recruiting is dishonest and that high school athletes themselves, and their families, are often guilty of encouraging abuses. Coaches, moreover, in facing the demeaning pressures of asking, persuading, cajoling seventeen-year-olds to accept a free education at a good university have been described as being little more than "pimps."[24] The analogy and its inevitable extension is, at best, disconcerting.

The seamy side of this whole sordid business, of course, is its effect on the young person at issue—and we are now only beginning to understand what might be called the plight of the student-athlete. Sought out almost entirely for athletic ability alone, seeing his persona reduced in the media to an almost commercial array of statistics (how many tackles, how many behind the line of scrimmage, how many, even, were shared with a teammate), the prospect more often than not will hear little about the educational possibilities and expectations of this or that institution.

Well, when you've hired this high school coach as a recruiter, he doesn't even know what degrees the university offers —sometimes the assistant coaches don't either—what they're talking to that boy and his family about in their living room a hundred miles from the campus is athletics, the team, the program—that's all.[25]

It would be unusual indeed for the winner of an athletic scholarship to State U., even one recruited with only minimal fanfare, to arrive as a freshman without a somewhat exalted sense of self-importance, an attitude that may well be sustained by the special treatment he receives, the elaborate facility in which he will live and eat being but the outward and visible sign. Sometimes this attitude will have a seriocomic dimension.

We're really doing student-athletes a disservice. We help them learn short circuits, shortcuts to getting things. And that's just not part of a good education for life. Somebody registers them, somebody goes and gets their books. I had a basketball player's mother call me to complain that the police were giving her son parking tickets. And I said, "Well, what lot does the sticker on his car allow him to park in?" She said, "He doesn't have a sticker," and I said, "He doesn't have a sticker?" She said, "No, he doesn't." I said, "Every other student on our campus is required to buy a parking permit to get a sticker that identifies what lots he can park in, and if he parks where he's supposed to be won't get a ticket." She then told me she didn't think he needed it. He was a basketball player.

There may well be among many student-athletes, especially those of star quality, a continuing attitude of such self-importance regarding responsibility for meeting institutional regulations. These attitudes can be reinforced by the widespread discriminatory practice in which athletes, in contrast to other students, have been routinely readmitted to good standing when they fall below established university requirements for continuation in residence but who meet the lesser conference or NCAA requirements for athletic eligibility. And there is some indication that the recognition factor attendant on highly visible sports participation leads to special considerations and favors for athletes among local businesses in collegiate settings and in competition for summer jobs.

There are notable exceptions, of course, but I can tell you from my conversations with many other CEOs who have had to deal with former athletes as alumni that for many of them that distortion of their role in society continues. In university fund-raising campaigns they hold a strong view that the institution owes them from now on, that they've already made their contribution.

But though we still know very little about either the specific short- or long-term social and emotional effects of athletic participation on student-athletes in later life, we are beginning to understand more fully the nature of their total undergraduate experience through research commissioned by the presidents commission of the NCAA. This research involved comparisons between more than four thousand student-athletes and other full-time students on forty-two campuses of Division I universities who were engaged in specific activities, such as the band or student newspaper, which required an important commitment of time.[26]

The research findings are not, perhaps, sufficient to dislodge the dumb-jock stereotype from the folklore of college sports, a character at least as old as James Thurber's gently satiric portrait, recalled from his Ohio State college days in 1915-1918, of Bolenciecwcz, the slow-witted tackle whom the entire economics class had to assist so he could play in the big game against Illinois.[27] But student-athletes of the 1980s typically major in business rather than "phizz-ed" and in many ways are quite comparable in attitude and experience with their nonathlete counterparts. For example, both groups are similar in the amount of time spent preparing for and attending class, in their apparent satisfaction with their academic experiences, and in their common belief that a college degree is a very important goal. However, athletes come to college less well prepared academically than other students and perform less well. Their graduation rates in the primary sports of football and basketball are significantly—in some sections of the country, dramatically—lower than those of the much more heterogeneous college population at large, although it might be observed that graduation rates in themselves do not tell a complete story.

> I've looked at transcripts of some athletes, kids who are potentially bright young men, and when I finish I want to cry. It hurts me to see them— even of people who have graduated—and I just realize that there's nothing in that transcript that you could give to a potential employer and say, "Look what I have acquired in my four years of college." That's the reason I have some hangups about this—I think we need more of our athletes to graduate, of course; but if graduation means these kinds of transcripts, I'm not for emphasis on that criterion.

Even a brief review of the responses reported in this research strongly suggests that the conditions of daily life encountered by student-athletes reinforce the actual and symbolic distance between their educational and athletic aspirations. Football and basketball players in more successfully competitive programs reported that even though academic support, such as personal or group tutoring, was more readily available to them than to other students, they found it more difficult to meet the demands of their academic schedules and to make academic work their highest priority. Obviously related to this response is the further indication that they experience many more problems with extreme tiredness or exhaustion than other student-athletes, a consequence of spending, in season, over an hour per day more than other athletes engaged directly in their sports—and two hours per day more in this way than nonathletes spent in their chosen extracurricular activities.   Moreover, but consistent with this pattern, measures of student conversational topics within their living quarters indicate that these same football and basketball players are heavily immersed in their sport off the field as well as on—and, though most student-athletes feel that living with other student-athletes is a good idea and enjoy the companionship of their peers, living in sequestered housing arrangements appears to be directly connected with reports from players in the two major sports that they more often experience feelings of isolation than those athletes living with other types of students.

Not only university presidents, but anyone genuinely interested in the healthy condition of intercollegiate athletics, should be greatly concerned about this combination of a lengthy playing schedule and off-season conditioning/weight-training programs in which many student-athletes participate, ostensibly on a voluntary basis. These year-round athletic activities require intense commitments of time and physical and mental energy. The resulting absorption of players with their sport and their concomitant sense of isolation often collide with the educational requirements and opportunities any student should primarily engage.

I think we deny athletes something by their not being part of the general student body, and I have known coaches who get terribly upset if an athlete pursues an interest in another area of the university.

When we've made a special admission exception for some athletes, knowing that they've developed their academic skills in a different fashion—put them to begin with in classroom competition at an unfair advantage, and then tie up their time extensively, we've just written a prescription for an academic problem.

For most students, undergraduate life is particularly characterized by that form of education that emerges silently and undramatically outside the classroom—in the new ideas one encounters, the opportunities for personal development, the extension of the persona through interaction with others. And again, anyone who sincerely cares about intercollegiate athletics, their relationship to the total university experience, and about the welfare of the young people who perform in these sports must feel a sense of unease at reports from student-athletes that they consistently and substantially feel less able than other students to acquire new abilities and skills, to assume leadership roles and a sense of responsibility for others, to set and achieve personal goals, to get to know other students, and to talk with others about their personal concerns and problems. And among the most poignant of the human dimensions lying behind these statistics is the revelation by all student-athletes, not just football and basketball players, about themselves in their responses as to whether it is "easier or harder for you, as a student-athlete/extracurricular activity student to . . . be liked by others for just being yourself":

TABLE *2.2* Percent Responding "Easier" or "Much Easier"

Football-Basketball	Other Sports	Extracurricular Activities
34.6	34.8	60.5

Undoubtedly the central and most authoritative figure in how student-athletes view their collegiate environment and their relationship to it is the coach. Student-athletes feel that of all the advisory or counseling roles a coach may fill, encouraging good performance in class and keeping track of this are by far the most important, their attitude on this being much stronger than that expressed by other students relative to their faculty activity advisors. Within the subgroup of football and basketball players, black student-athletes in both predominantly white and predominantly black institutions had stronger feelings about this type of academic motivation than did members of the grouping as a whole. It is encouraging to note from this research that approximately one-third of all football and basketball players and one-third of black players in these sports rated their coaches as "excellent" in this area. However, it is even more important—and discouraging—to see that the other two-thirds of all student-athletes rated their coaches as "fair," "poor," or "terrible."

> *Coaches, I know, have a lot of pressure on them. But in the main, they're not natural adherents to higher education. I don't mean to knock them at all, but I mean they come from different backgrounds; they don't immediately associate with the ethos of the institution. I don't worry much about a dean or professor because they have been brought up and live their lives inside an environment which I share—and therefore I can tell them to remember what it is that academics do, what we think about. But when we talk about incorporating the athletic side of the house into the institution's ethos, we have to recognize they do very different things. If you've got this basic separation, well, you hire a CEO who's, say, a physician—an expert on kidney disease and you tell him over there you've got to treat cancer. Now you can either retrain the CEO or you can change the view of the nature of the healthy organism over there. In that latter case the organism to be fully healthy has to be a part of the university ethos. . . . I sit with coaches all the time. I want to know*

everything they do — how they live their lives and I want them to know how I live mine and what my business is about. I think they hate me.

The "inside-over there," "two-sides-of-the-house" images that mark this presidential statement are, of course, synonymous with the loss-of-memory figure used earlier in this chapter to describe the two-cultures condition that separates the athletic organ from the larger body of higher education. It is fair to say that universities, unlike the efforts of this CEO, have not done enough or found ways to bring athletic coaching staffs into direct and continuing contact with the academic environment, its values and modes of conduct. And coaches, who now rarely hold faculty appointments, have perhaps not sufficiently realized their considerable opportunity to be teachers, to "profess" the values of an ethos that, in fact, encircles the daily lives of their players.

The need for the potentially tempering voice of the coach is obvious when one perceives the unrealistic expectations of many black football and basketball players for becoming professional athletes. Approximately 14 percent of these players at predominantly white institutions and 24 percent at predominantly black institutions who stated this objective were second-team or third-team players. Of equal significance in likely mismatches between ability levels and career objectives, about 35 percent and 22 percent of these discrete groups who stated they would almost certainly attend graduate or professional school had earned GPAs less than a level of C.

There surely are powerful external forces at work, especially in Division I-A schools, that may inhibit coaches from securing a genuine sense of institutional identity, seeing the team and its territorial energy as part of a continuous domain of reciprocal values. Coaches *do* care for their players, of course, about their futures, and are positive influences in shaping their educational perspectives. But, even though there are exceptions, the evidence thus far is not persuasive to indicate that both sides of the institutional house speak the same language or share an understanding of which language should be primary.

I wondered why the coach, whom I didn't know well at all, had asked for the appointment. He had said something about a favor for a member of the team who was in my class that term. He got right to the point. The player in question was the first-team quarterback. He had great potential for professional football, said the coach. But he needed a B grade in my class to be eligible to compete on Saturday, which was extremely important for his pro career. The boy had missed class frequently, hadn't completed assignments properly, and had no grade higher than C. I wasn't trying to be clever, but I responded that I, too, would like a favor of him for another student I had — one who was soon to graduate, and a Rhodes Scholarship candidate. Could you do him a favor, I asked. Maybe. It would help his candidacy greatly if he could be the starting quarterback in the game on Saturday. He rose at once and our parting was reasonably amiable but quick.

This conversation took place during the recent past, at an eminent Division I-A institution. And, in its recollection by the faculty member himself, now a senior administrator in another prestigious public university, it illustrates once more the potentially fatal separation between the game and the environment that permits its existence.

The causes and conditions of that separation between athletics and academe may, as we have seen, be metaphorically illuminated in terms of a language difficulty, a memory loss, the relationship between disease and its causative agents, or, in sociohistoric terms, as the natural tendency of athletics to assume—with widespread public approval—many of the characteristics inherent in the cultural forces that initially stimulated their movement away from their sponsoring environment. But however the separation may be explained or described, it has been present for over a century, can no longer be suppressed, and is steadily eroding the image of higher education as the principal secular institution holding together a configuration of past, present, and future in a kind of public trust. Our appraisal of the condition of college sports has often emphasized a preservation of their exciting and dramatic public presence and the multiple values that accrue to us, the audience, through our symbolic participation in that presence. But as we now turn to a proposed prescription for reform and its possibilities for truly becoming a "coping mechanism," it is critical that we keep in mind the essential concerns that have led us to this point: however valuable those messages are that college sports communicate to millions of Americans, at what human and ethical costs are they being sent, and, on our part, at what level of impersonality to those costs are they being received?

NOTES

1. The source for all illustrative statistics on penalties and violations is *NCAA Enforcement Summary*. This document is available from NCAA, 6201 College Boulevard, Overland Park, KS 66221-2422. Details about specific cases are from the pertinent *News Release* issued by the NCAA at the time of announcement of the penalties imposed on the institution by the Committee on Infractions.
2. See L. Jay Oliva, "A Special Message to Division III," Chapter 10 of *What Trustees Should Know About Intercollegiate Athletics* (Washington, DC: Association of Governing Boards of Universities and Colleges, 1989). The "message" is a warning to CEOs to be aware of the very types of abuses described immediately below, even though such abuses may be "petty larceny in a world of big-time crime."

3. This pattern is meticulously illustrated in *The Bishops' Committee Report on SMU, Friday, June 19, 1987: Report to the Board of Trustees of Southern Methodist University from the Special Committee of Bishops of the South Central Jurisdiction of the United Methodist Church* (Dallas: United Methodist Reporter, 1987).

4. Robert A. Nisbet, *Social Change and History* (New York: Oxford University Press, 1969), p. 6.

5. The scientific term for this concept is "multifactorial etiology." The classic treatise is Rene J. Dubos, *Mirage of Health: Utopias, Progress, and Biological Change* (New York: Harper's, 1959). The illustrative fever-blister analogy comes from a paper by Dubos for nonscientists, "Second Thoughts on the Germ Theory," *Scientific American*, 192 (May 1955), pp. 31-35.

6. Although fraudulent manipulations of research data usually are not based on an economic rationale, research achievements are themselves directly connected to the economic conditions—low salaries and heavy work loads—surrounding the employment of graduate teaching assistants, junior laboratory associates, medical interns, and residents. Such conditions are largely obscured—because of their place as an "academic tradition"—but the university's exploitation of such young professionals is uncomfortably analogous to the economic exploitation of student athletes.

7. The *Memorandum to the 41st President of the United States* was developed by the Committee on National Challenges in Higher Education (Washington, DC: American Council on Education, 1989). See also Derek Bok, *The President's Report, 1986-1987, Harvard University*, for a review of university efforts since the 1970s to incorporate the study of "moral reasoning" into the undergraduate curriculum.

8. This presidential observation finds a correlative parallel in new research on the statistical relationship between the significant erosion of productivity growth rates in the 1970s and 1980s and the unprecedented decline, beginning in 1967, of student test scores measuring GIA ("general intellectual achievement," related to productivity in most jobs). See John H. Bishop, "Is the Test Score Decline Responsible for the Productivity Growth Decline?" *The American Economic Review* 79 (March 1989), pp. 178-197.

9. See James Santomier and Peter Cautilli, "Controlling Deviance in College Sports," in *Sport and Higher Education*, ed. Donald Chu, et al. (Champaign, IL: Human Kinetics, 1985), pp. 297-404.

10. "Division I, II, and III Philosophy Statements," *NCAA Manual, 1989-1990* (Mission, KS: National Collegiate Athletic Association, March 1989), pp. 282, 288, 291-292.

11. Donna Lopiano offers a different view in "Guest Editorial: A Speech Made at the NCAA Presidents Commission National Forum, June 1987," *Physical Educator*, 45(1) (Winter 1988), pp. 2-4. She describes the athletic activity as a "performing art" comparable to student performance in the college theater or symphony, and in its "nonclassroom setting . . . no different than the practicum of the student newspaper." While the student may indeed secure from all of these a genuine sense of personal development, the remoteness of athletics from the established curriculum makes such analogies tenuous as justification for their receipt of

current levels of institutional commitments of time and money. A practicum is a laboratory setting where the theory of classroom instruction is tested and practiced under faculty supervision within the construct of the student's academic major—journalism in the example cited. There is no academic major in athletics.

12. James A. Michener, *Sports in America* (New York: Random House, 1976), p. 11.

13. See Lee Sigelman and Robert Carter, "Alumni Giving and Big-time College Sports," *Social Science Quarterly* 60 (September 1979), pp. 284-294, and James H. Frey, "The Winning-Team Myth," *Currents* 11 (January 1985), pp. 32-35. This conclusion is reenforced in a more recent and extensive survey of research and informed university opinion on the subject: see Douglas Lederman, "Do Winning Teams Spur Contributions? Scholars and Fund Raisers Are Skeptical," *Chronicle of Higher Education* 34 (January 13, 1988), pp. A1, 32-34.

14. Dave Anderson, *New York Times* (January 15, 1989).

15. Mitchell Raiborn, *NCAA News* (January 20, 1988), p. 6. Data presented by Raiborn have been arranged here in tabular form for ease of comparison.

16. In all fairness to coaches, who can hardly be expected to turn down such largesse, it should be noted that the consultative activity of university faculty through which large supplementary incomes often accrue is also for many universities a troubling ethical issue that has commercial dimensions. Such activity can usually be justified as sustaining the university mission of public service and enhancing the faculty member's own competence for performing the teaching-research duties funded by the institution. The relative size and sources of the two supplementary incomes, however, would seem to be less important than the difference between the carefully regulated prohibition on the one hand of a faculty consultant in any way assuming an institutional identity and the frank exploitation on the other of institutional symbols, logos, facilities, and even students, for the marketing of commercial products with the coach as the central spokesman for the products.

17. See James H. Frey, "Boosterism, Scarce Resources, and Institutional Control: The Future of American Intercollegiate Athletics," in Chu, et al., ed., *Sport and Higher Education*, p. 119. The larger body of the university itself is not isolated from charges of commercialism, in its marketing of research services, for example, in competition with the private sector. See Burton A. Weisbrod, *The Nonprofit Economy* (Cambridge, MA: Harvard University Press, 1988), pp. 110-112. Such actions are essentially designed to secure funds to finance institutional missions of research and teaching, but, as Weisbrod observes, they actually serve only to erode the integrity of an institution's educational mission and actually endanger its support from the business sector. The parallel with athletic programs is striking.

18. Quoted in Guy Maxton Lewis, "The American Intercollegiate Football Spectacle, 1869-1917," (Ph.D. diss., University of Maryland, 1965), p. 270.

19. The NCAA, as other regulatory organizations connected with sports competition at all levels have done, has defined the distinction between "amateur" and "professional," the former status being lost when an athlete "receives, directly or indirectly, any kind of payment (including awards, benefits and expenses) for athletic participation except as permitted by the association's governing legislation," which is quite detailed. A useful survey of the long and complicated social history of the concept of amateurism in sports may be found in Ronald A. Smith, *Sports and Freedom: The Rise of Big-Time College Athletics* (New York: Oxford

University Press, 1988). The complex issue of financial aid to athletes is discussed in chapter 3.

20. The "self-generated" thesis can be applied beyond the Division I-A environment:

> *The motivation to cheat is very strong at our Division II level and ethical corners are definitely being cut because many of our young coaches just want to be in Division I.*

> *I've watched some of the coaches, they're good guys, good gals, but they have this notion "I'm here for a few years only." They come in, anxious to go higher and just think and talk Division I. I hear them ask why can't our athletes have this special tutoring so they can spend more time on the field? I think what is this? A few coaches are really of Division I caliber but they like our Division III philosophy and want to stay. But I don't see too many of them.*

21. See David Riesman and Reuel Denny, "Football in America: A Study in Culture Diffusion," in *The Sporting Image*, ed. Paul J. Zingg (Lanham, MD: University Press of America, 1988), pp. 209-226.

22. The institutionalizing of women's sports is, of course, the final stage.

23. See David Riesman, "Ten Years On: The Higher Learning in America Since the Events of 1968," *New Republic* (July 1, 1978), pp. 13-17.

24. Bo Schembechler and Mitchell Albom, *Bo* (New York: Warner Books, 1989), p. 229.

25. Lest this comment be misconstrued, NCAA regulations permit, under certain conditions, a high-school coach to be employed by a Division III institution and to engage in recruiting.

26. All comparative statistics in the text below are taken from two of the studies commissioned by the NCAA and conducted by the Center for the Study of Athletics, American Institutes for Research, Palo Alto, CA: Report 1, *Summary Results from the 1987-1988 National Study of Intercollegiate Athletics* (November 1988), and Report 3, *Experiences of Black Intercollegiate Athletes at NCAA Division I Institutions* (March 1989).

27. James Thurber, "University Days," *My Life and Hard Times* (New York: Harper's, 1933), pp. 115-120. This stereotype, and his counterpart in professional sports, still lives a satiric life in the widely syndicated comic strip "Tank McNamara."

Chapter 3

Prescription for Reform: The Essential Ingredients

> *Every generation seems to think we're going to the dogs in respect to our traditional values of education. I don't agree with that. I think there's a higher sensitivity to ethics now than there has been in the last several decades—part of this is simply a product of mass communication. Our consciousness level is raised when the probability of exposure is very high, and you're seeing what has happened in athletics on the front pages every day. Behavior is behavior, whether in athletics, the Congress, or the big corporations—but I'll tell you one thing: a framework of law is essential if human behavior is to be changed. The civil rights and voting rights acts in the 1960s may not necessarily have changed individual attitudes or feelings about one group or another but they changed our public behavior—and it was by an overwhelming consensus, not just a two-thirds majority in the Senate, that the nation got that message of change. It might have been painful and upset a lot of people but we achieved a little progress in this world, and I believe the same principle applies in intercollegiate athletics. . . . The whole purpose of the NCAA is to secure a consensus legislative plan on the ground rules to guide amateurism and its values in an ethical sense. And the question is: are we going to obey them? Sure, I know everybody wants to abolish the NCAA, but we all know we'd have to create something like it the very next day. So why don't we try to improve what we're working with now?*

This extensive, thoughtful comment by a university president links together much of what has been set forth in the first half of this book about the condition of intercollegiate athletics and those proposals for improving its health that will constitute the second half. The statement also, through its analogy between the problems of college sports and those inherent in the great social drama of the last thirty years, reaffirms in a sense this book's basic premise: that an understanding of fundamental and secondary causes of the condition are requisite to any relevant program of reform, and that the means of reform can indeed emerge from within the present governance structure. The potential for this seems inherent from the conjunction in the present time between the nationally renewed ethical sensitivity and the attention now directed to the imbalance between academics and athletics. One might observe, ironically, that this awareness is heightened by the same intense emphasis in the media that has itself been partially responsible for the disproportionate place college athletics have assumed within the culture.

It is not at all clear, of course, just what the connection may be between cheating in the world of college sports and widely publicized scandals in government and the corporate state. On the one hand, there may be no significant ethical distinction between betrayals of the public trust by an elected official or of stockholders by a corporate executive and the denial of those educational values that define a university's very existence by a coach or alumnus who arranges the bribery of a 250-pound linebacker who runs a 4.5. On the other hand, universities, as we have seen, are not fundamentally animated by the profit motive and consistently oppose the public tendency to make them mirrors of society and its pragmatic ethos. Yet no matter how many athletic programs throughout the country are untainted by scandal, the daily disclosures of greed, brutality, and corruption in others seem to have fixed firmly in the public mind a linkage between corruption in intercollegiate athletics and that in other realms of the national life.

The university is peculiarly vulnerable to charges of hypocrisy and devious behavior in its conduct of any program bearing its representational identity, although the university in American life, until now, has not been dramatically required to answer such charges. Inside traders can be sent to jail and new public officials can be elected. But universities are hampered by the relatively low interest of the public in their educational mission. Also, some would argue that because of their own indigenous decentralized form of governance, universities do not possess the recuperative ability to refute the claim that they are at the mercy of a subculture with alien values, one that is closely linked to ominous forms of wealth, egocentricity, and political power.

To some, given this perceived state of affairs, the prognosis is so bleak that only one treatment of the disease seems practical: amputation—that is, removing athletics from the administration and responsibility of the university body. Such an operation might take the form of widespread transfers from universities to private enterprise, either through leasing or selling of athletic facilities not needed for student instruction or recreation. Teams would be sponsored by sports clubs, somewhat on the European model, with players who are also students receiving compensation just like nonstudent players.

Another form of overt separation would be to abandon the current code that regulates the level of financial aid student-athletes may receive and to pay salaries derived from athletic revenues directly to the players, salaries that might be well in excess of the full costs of the student's annual enrollment, and that might even be assigned in terms of a given player's relative value to the team. Or, as yet another proposal argues, a new class of student-athletes might qualify for admission to four-year institutions, their only credentials being high-school graduation and a requisite level of athletic talent. Their special curriculum would take two directions: first, instruction in practical matters pertinent to a potential future in professional sports—such as managing personal finance, working with sports agents, lawyers, and accountants, and responding to the news media—and, second, instruction in basic reading, writing, and mathematics along with training in service occupations that might lead to long-term employment.[1]

At first glance, proposals of this kind may be attractive, but on further consideration they seem abortive, farfetched, and enormously difficult to implement. It is most unlikely that hundreds of institutions would agree to commit themselves publicly to an overtly commercial pay-for-play system, and many legal and financial problems would accrue from the presence of privately owned franchises conducting business in leased institutional facilities in the middle of university campuses, where sports stadiums and arenas are typically located.[2]

> *Once you admit it's a professional franchise and not part of the educational process, you lose all your tax advantages. Paying ad valorem taxes on a stadium and corporate income taxes on net profit would decimate much of the supposedly huge profits athletic programs enjoy. They would just disappear in the mire of taxes.*

Yet, proposals like these all reflect a kind of rough honesty. They assume that the typical financial-aid support given to student-athletes in itself is a commercial transaction—the payment of wages for services rendered—and thus no ethical contradiction would exist were student athletes to share more fully in the financial revenues their services help to produce. Moreover, any form of removing the troublesome subculture of athletics from the host would allow universities to free themselves from an intolerable conflict of interest wherein the same administrative system that attempts to create an ethical environment in which the discovery and transmission of knowledge may flourish must also carry the burden of a costly sports enterprise whose purposes, modes of conduct, and claims on student participants appear to have little if anything to do with the educational values of the institution. All of this indirectly affirms the diagnosis offered in the previous chapter, since each proposal for control of abuses would neutralize certain economic and egocentric drives that may function as secondary causes in the complex anatomy of infractions, exciting a fundamental corruption of the university's educational mission and ethical commitment.

A further rationale for subverting and recasting the current financial relationship between university and student-athlete is the view that this arrangement discriminates against all student-athletes but especially against those who may have been educationally and economically disadvantaged and for whom college sports offer a social mobility not otherwise available. One might argue, of course, that many a disadvantaged young person who cannot run, jump, shoot, or tackle at a high level of skill and efficiency would love to have the room and board, tuition, books, and other assistance his athletically gifted peers receive, to say nothing of their opportunity. Yet the matter of financial aid to student-athletes remains a problematic issue.

> *If we recruit a kid who's really poor, comes from a large family, there's got to be a way for that level of student-athlete to come to a campus like this, mostly middle-class students, and not have to live like a pauper and it not be illegal. His scholarship and Pell grant may be just enough that he's not embarrassed about his clothes and all that, but if he also feels he's got to be helping out the family he left behind, I think that creates a crisis in intercollegiate athletics.*

It is not particularly helpful, however, to assign discriminatory status to student-athletes whose participation in financial and commercial activities is curtailed by the provisions of their scholarships while comparing them to other students whose scholarships, based on different forms of talent, contain no such prohibitions.[3] It is true that a student holding a scholarship based on musical talent, or a French or mathematics major holding an academic scholarship, may well augment his or her financial status by, for example, playing for musical groups inside or outside the institution or by charging certain rates for conducting tutorials. But in so doing, such students "market" only themselves and their own abilities; in this sense they are somewhat like the faculty member who, as noted earlier, in consultantships with business or industry must carry only his or her scientific or intellectual identity. The faculty member is, in fact, contractually constrained from representing the institution in any way and from using its resources for personal gain without appropriate compensation. The participation in the commercial marketing of products by a student-athlete, whose identity is irrevocably connected with membership on an athletic team sponsored by the university (and part of whose educational costs in state institutions is supported by public funds), would inevitably associate the university directly with the acts of advertising, buying, and selling. Admittedly, this is a fine point of distinction but the principle at issue should not be misconstrued. It might be observed, however, once more ironically, that the one figure in the collegiate setting whose public identity is most fully marked by the athletic connection, the coach, is rarely constrained in any way from utilizing institutional symbols, or even property, in the advertising and promotion of goods for personal profit. (For further discussion of this aspect of coaches' compensation, see the section "Finances" in chap. 4.)

But however attractive the overt translation of intercollegiate athletics into a commercial enterprise may appear to be, such an act could yield a devastating sense of loss. What might be lost may in fact be an illusion—that is, the illusion that intercollegiate athletics sustains a vague concept of amateurism in which participation is motivated not by financial gain but by the joy of competition and its challenges to the body and spirit. A number of perceptive and learned discourses have pretty well debunked the historical validity of this tradition in the Western world, illustrating instead that the economically untainted concept of amateurism had its origins in social discrimination, distinguishing in the matter of games "gentlemen" from members of the laboring class.[4]

However, it is entirely another matter as to whether the current regulation of intercollegiate athletics is now an anachronism, hypocritically clinging to a concept of amateurism long known to lack validity and thereby keeping student-athletes in a kind of economic bondage even though their athletic efforts annually produce untold millions of dollars in revenue. To be sure, there may be a certain discomfort in our awareness that the student athlete under the current NCAA-approved grant-in-aid system is indeed being supported at a certain financial level in return for services rendered. And we would be looking the other way not to admit that the regimentation of the student-athlete's life in the form of mandatory practices and other forms of discipline is a requirement of that financial support, a requirement that goes beyond the normal expectations of other scholarship undergraduates who, to sustain their financial aid, must ordinarily only pursue their degrees at a certain pace and academic level of achievement.

But is this condition an illusion, a shimmering ideal based on hypocrisy and a false sense of the history of sport? Perhaps—but probably not. After all, intercollegiate athletics has been regulated and had its principles of fairness and equity interpreted by the NCAA for over eighty years, and its defined system of financial aid to student-athletes has been in place since the mid 1950s. That system may indeed be less than ideal, and the concept of amateurism that it defines certainly is flawed in the absolute definition of that term. Yet it would surely be strange if that differentiation were not already recognized among the millions of Americans whose restless energy responds to college sports in such powerful ways.

Our history is filled with the discovery of flawed ideals that within the democratic process have been reformed and accommodated. And it might be observed that ideals do have a tendency to shimmer when we are in danger of being separated from them. Testimony from every front confirms that abuses of greed and self-interest are now placing extraordinary stress on the linkage between games, undergraduate students, and the secular cathedrals of higher education, a linkage that Americans apparently wish to remain securely intact. There is, of course, no scientific evidence to bolster this latter affirmation. Still, a poll published recently in a popular weekly and involving over thirty-one thousand respondents who were identified as being highly supportive of collegiate and professional athletics is at least a straw in the winds of opinion. Over three-fourths of those polled flatly rejected the concept that college athletes should be paid.[5] And by implication also, such respondents would find a melancholy contradiction in watching an athletic performance on a university campus between teams that were owned by private interests, whose existence had no link— either real or symbolic—with the spires and towers of the educational buildings visible beyond the rim of the stadium, and whose efficiency might be marred by the absence of two or three key players who are not injured but have not yet agreed with management on the terms of their contracts. (For further discussion of financial aid for student-athletes, see the section "Finances" in chapter 4.)

If not the ultimate treatment of amputation, then, how can higher education build on the "little progress" that has been made and move toward the control of a disease that, though latent in some quarters, remains severe and deeply entrenched in the population? Obviously it is impossible within the milieu of intercollegiate athletics to eliminate all actions that flow from human motivations of pride, misplaced values, and self-interest, which in the diagnosis set forth earlier tend to corrupt the basic educational mission of the university. Given the uneasy history of the relationship between these two cultures and the differentiations marking their existence, which have become increasingly clarified in the last twenty-five years, it may be that we should anticipate no more than a condition of watchful coexistence, a kind of symbiosis in which two different species of organisms live together in close relationship. Sustaining for a moment the language of biology, however, a reasonably optimistic prognosis is justified only if the symbiotic relationship called "parasitism" is neutralized—where one party benefits but the other is harmed—and that called "mutualism" becomes dominant—where both parties benefit by the connection.[6]

That the motivation necessary to achieve this condition is beginning to emerge among the diverse constituencies of the NCAA is evident from some of their responses during the 1980s to the complex pathology of infractions. Higher academic standards have been adopted by Divisions I and II for both freshman eligibility and progress toward a degree. The membership has imposed more severe penalties for major violations, some of which, a significant reduction in the number of athletic scholarships, for example, may adversely affect a program far beyond the penalty period itself. A revision of the *NCAA Manual* was completed to assist institutional staff members acquire a better working knowledge of the association's regulations.[7] A presidents commission was established within the NCAA structure with a charge to exert stronger presidential leadership in controlling and maintaining a proper compatibility between college sports and higher education. The results of detailed and lengthy research efforts sponsored by the NCAA, such as those on the welfare of student-athletes cited in chapter 2, are beginning to provide solidly objective reference points for legislative action. Likewise, the ten-year study on the academic performance of student-athletes in Division I (which will be completed in 1994) will provide data for the appropriate modification of eligibility requirements. Finally, and perhaps of greatest significance, the membership has demonstrated by these actions and in other ways a willingness to address forthrightly its problems and to make changes.

The possibility for further and perhaps more dramatic legislative changes on the national scene now seem imminently possible during the 1990s, as will be discussed in chapter 4. And though such changes will be necessary to increase the momentum of reform from the "little progress" now under way, the critical stage of action in the development of an effective prescription for the control of abuses will continue to be the home front, the university setting itself. It appears likely that the faculty will play a more significant role than in the past, as they should, given the stake they have in the academic integrity of the university. However, the featured players will still be the university president, the governing board, the athletic director, the head coach, and, of course, that transient population whose games form the text of the play: the student-athletes themselves.

THE ROLE OF THE UNIVERSITY PRESIDENT

I know this is going to sound facetious, but it really isn't: if any person is interested in becoming president or chancellor of a Division I-A institution and he or she doesn't like football, then that person better look for a job somewhere else; because you've just got to spend an awful lot of time at it. The intercollegiate athletic program is not something you can leave for someone else to take care of.

Any meaningful prognosis for achieving a guarded yet truly reciprocal symbiosis between higher education and college sports must depend heavily on the leadership, values, and courage of the university president, whose job is widely misunderstood and perhaps badly underrated in its complexity. As leader of the faculty, the president's academic standards and vision for the institution are under constant internal scrutiny. And as principal interpreter of the institution to its many constituencies, the president must know absolutely the pulse of the one program that is by far the university's most public:

I mean the math department and the history department don't appear in the newspaper every day, but your athletic program does, and there are people going around trying to find something to write about it. You've got to pay attention to it.

Its public visibility is one thing, but, as we have seen, the silent and ominous power of sports programs to forge linkages with centers of economic and political influence is another element any candidate for a university presidency should perceive.

Under the NCAA constitution, the institutional president "has ultimate responsibility and final authority for the conduct of the intercollegiate athletics program." This point of authority, while legislatively clear and incontrovertible, is often ambiguously communicated, to both university faculty and public, when institutions at times of crisis or significant change in the athletic program seem represented not by the president but by the governing board or even by the athletic director. Unfortunately, the agreement on the president's authority in these matters is not always secured explicitly with the governing board at the time of appointment, perhaps due to the unjustified assumption that the point is already understood or to the fact that many individuals are promoted, as it were, into the office of president without any significant experience in the administration of athletics and thus are not aware of the critical importance of this issue.

Just this morning I had the chance to talk with a younger colleague about whether he should take the presidency at an institution—which I knew a lot about—and I told him, "If you don't get from that board of trustees that you have the right to either continue or discontinue the employment of anyone on that campus, including the head football or basketball coach, if you have clear evidence there would be a serious problem if you did terminate them, then you'd better not go."

During my interview process I raised some of the questions [about administrative control of athletics] and got very generalized answers which, on reflection as I look back now, were not nearly specific enough. So three or four months into this role I asked for and received from our board a very specific statement of delegation of responsibility for intercollegiate athletics, and I've used that since to remind a couple of folks that that is an institutional matter; that's not a matter for individual board members.

This latter president was not only perceptive but also fortunate. The average presidential tenure in major universities currently is less than five years, the early portion of which is customarily spent in traveling around to meet new constituencies and establishing relationships with faculty and academic administrators. If the authority for athletic decision-making is not secured early in the administrative period, it may be too late to get it without confrontation should the latent disease of corruption be unexpectedly incited by secondary causes. If such a crisis should occur, or should difficulties arise from situations such as those documented ones where, for example, a coach was hired by a governing board before the new president's appointment, or the athletic director had been hired through the strong sponsorship of a head coach, then

> *Some chief executive officers are just going to have to lose their jobs. That's the bottom line of this whole enterprise. It's easy for me to say because I'm not going to be one of them at this point; but I've been recruited during this past year by two major Division I institutions and it was clear to me that athletic problems were going to be an issue right off the bat. . . . I believe that these things can't be handled diplomatically. In the end the chief officer has to say, "Look, friends, there's a way we're not going to run this place. I'm not looking for trouble, but I'm telling you I want to meet my responsibilities and I can't meet them in the way you guys are operating. Now you can either have me as your president or you can get somebody else." Now that's tough, but what other remedy is there to a basic structural question of who's in charge of the program? You say, "What happens to people like that?" Well, _____ lost his job at _____, came to _____. Where is he now? He's chancellor at _____. He took a punch in the course of all that, but no one in higher education thinks any less of him for it. . . . Why some presidents seem reluctant to lose their jobs over athletics, I don't know. It's a badge of honor these days.*

Perhaps the most important single action the university president can take to prevent crisis administration in the athletic program is to see that an institutional position paper is developed and fully communicated. Although the basic elements of this position paper are now required by the NCAA as a part of the institutional self-study conducted at five-year intervals, the document can serve a purpose far beyond that required for eligibility for participation in NCAA championships or for historical record-keeping, becoming a standard of reference by which the administration of athletics is guided and evaluated. The position statement should, of course, begin with a clear commitment of the president to his or her responsibility under NCAA legislation and the pattern of involvement that commitment will take. The practice of one CEO merits special emphasis here:

> *As the CEO of this institution, I meet once a year with every person employed in men's and women's athletics . . . anybody who draws a*

paycheck in intercollegiate athletics; and they are told in a very serious way that anyone who knowingly violates NCAA rules will be fired. I say that decision has been made and ask "Does everyone understand it?" I make no humor about it and look around the room in a very serious way. I never get a question. After that I write each of them a letter that says anyone who knowingly violates NCAA rules will be fired.

There should never be any question about the institution's policy on athletics if the document also sets forth:

- The goals and objectives of the program, which should be realistic with respect to the resources available for the various sports in regard to the levels of competition to be achieved
- The process for development and review of policies governing the athletic program
- The administrative structure for management of the program
- Academic standards for student-athletes, with explicit reference to any provisions for special admission or retention, and information about academic support programs available for student-athletes
- The nature of the institution's commitment to the physical, social, and emotional welfare of the student-athletes, and identification of resources for keeping this commitment
- Procedures for internal monitoring of the program for rules compliance and academic integrity
- A statement of the ways in which the institution will keep all its constituencies informed of its pledge to operate its athletic program in keeping with established policies and governing legislation

This latter element is an especially critical point in reassuring the faculty and staff just what the living conditions are for the "other side" of the institutional house, and publication of elements of the document in the periodic alumni magazine or newsletter provides an excellent way of preventing misunderstandings among athletic-support groups.

As indicated above, the policy and procedures for monitoring of the athletic program constitute an important element in the institutional position paper on athletics, and it is one to which the CEO should assign high priority. For control of abuses in college sports, this activity is comparable to epidemiological surveillance, an essential component in effective disease control.

Program monitoring is just a basic management tool for compliance review that we ought to use in the athletic area like we do in every other area. All managements use CPAs and that is not a reflection on your accounting staff or lack of concern about internal control, but an action to build comfort level. Monitoring the athletic program is not an indictment of the credibility of the athletic leadership—we're saying "Here is another tool for you to use as well as the athletic administration to ensure that we have an educational capability and a detection capability that is quasi-independent of any given function."

Many factors combine to make rigorous monitoring for rules compliance necessary. They can be summarized as follows:

- The regulations governing intercollegiate athletics are numerous and, in many instances, complex.
- The institution is responsible for every decision and action taken by members of its staff, by its student-athletes, and by representatives of its athletic interests.
- The stakes are too high to risk having improprieties or inadvertent mistakes go undetected.[8]

Each institution must determine the most appropriate mechanism for monitoring its athletic program. However, in most institutions with big-time sports programs it is imperative that there be explicit provision for monitoring the program by an official outside the athletic department who reports directly to the chief executive officer in fulfilling this responsibility. In recent years, an increasing number of institutions have established full-time positions for "directors of compliance," most of these within the athletic department. Such a position can be very effective in helping the athletic director administer the program with greater assurance of compliance with all institutional, conference, and NCAA regulations. The greater the care given to the administration of a program within the department, the less need there will be for extensive monitoring from outside; but that external monitoring is essential for all big-time sports programs.

While emphasis in the monitoring program has traditionally focused primarily on rules compliance,[9] to be truly effective it must place equal emphasis on the integrity of the academic program. The proper division of responsibility for these activities (i.e., the administrator for rules compliance and the faculty for academic integrity) should be explicit in the institution's position on its athletic program.

Fortunately, testimony from interviews with university presidents make it clear that those of their colleagues who would take shortcuts and subordinate institutional integrity are very much in the minority. Still, to return to the observation with which this section began, the current realities of university administration argue strongly that the tenure of a president—and not only those serving institutions with big-time sports programs—will not be successful if he or she adopts a *laissez-faire* or patronizing attitude toward the athletic scene.

> *Would a president say to a dean, "Listen, I don't care whom you give tenure to, that's your business." Would he say that? If he would, he's not doing his business. If he says to the chief financial officer, "Look I don't care what you're doing with the money, just make sure everything's fine." Baloney! He wants to know week by week the financial state of the place — how the budget is made, how the money is being expended. And as soon as you get to the athletic end of the spectrum—blank. That's probably the most serious part of our business!*

Thus perhaps the most urgent content of the institutional position paper will be that describing the level of visibility and involvement of the president— and how he or she will manage that commitment. In a sense, all will move outward from this.

> *If I had to put my finger on the really important relationship in intercollegiate athletics, it would be put on the president's connection to the program. The leaders of institutions have to view themselves in a sense as physicians because diagnosis of an athletic problem or condition is so important. What, it seems to me, we have to work on is who's going to do that. With what skill, with what understanding will a physician approach the problem? The old style physicians used to make house calls, and I think today that's what university athletics need: physicians who are willing to make house calls.*

THE ROLE OF THE GOVERNING BOARD

Far too little emphasis has been placed on the role of governing boards, who have a truly critical role to play in stopping corruption in college sports.

The importance of the governing board's role is best understood by drawing on our analogy of abuses in college sports as a disease of higher education. An endemic disease can be brought under control only when wise policies and well-designed strategic plans have been developed, when commitment for control is made at the top and communicated through the chain of command to the field forces, and when the plan is implemented properly by workers in the field having day-to-day contact with the population who are the primary recipients of treatment or preventive measures. Appro- priate resources must also be provided to achieve success in the control program. These principles are applicable to the control of abuses in intercollegiate athletics.

Even though the CEO is held responsible for the control of abuses in an institution's athletic program, he or she cannot design and implement an effective control program without the full support of the governing board, whose role can be stated in both positive and negative terms. The board should affirm commitment that the institution will conduct with integrity an intercollegiate athletic program that places emphasis on the proper relationship of athletics and education and that the board will support the CEO fully in achieving this objective, but the board should not intrude into the administration of the program.

The way in which the board functions in the governance of intercollegiate athletics will be determined by its general approach to its responsibilities. In their recent extensive study of what governing boards do and how well they do it, Clark Kerr and Marian Gade identified nine generalized types of boards and found near universal agreement that the most satisfactory model was a type designated as an "overall policy and performance board," which "gives more or less equal attention to all major aspects of policy and of performance. . . . It does not try to administer. It respects the role of the faculty. It protects autonomy and academic freedom alike. It selects and supports able presidents. . . . It concentrates on results."[10]

This description of the most satisfactory model for governing boards provides insight about reasons the board should not intrude into the administration of an institution's athletic program—its most visible element. To intrude into the management of athletics demonstrates lack of support for the president, lack of respect for the role of the faculty, and a distortion of institutional priorities.

Governing board members are more likely to become directly involved with an athletic program when the board governs a single institution than when it governs a statewide system. In the most extreme cases, governing boards assume responsibility for selection of the coach or athletic director, or the state governor uses his or her power over the board to accomplish this or to negotiate a contract directly with the coach. Experiences in a number of institutions over the past decade make it abundantly clear that the responsibility for administration of the athletic program should properly be delegated to the president, with full authority to control every aspect of the program, as expressed emphatically by one experienced CEO:

The ideal situation is to not have your board mucking around in athletics. The only way that you are going to stop that from happening is to be willing to put your job on the line. If you ever compromise on that, if you ever open the door and allow them to get involved in athletics, then they are likely to drive the whole program crazy. So it has to be a very clear understanding that as long as you are the president, board members are not allowed to mess around in athletics.

Because of the visibility of the athletic program, its influence on the perceptions about the institution and the keen interest in athletics by various constituencies of the institution, it is only natural for members of a governing board to have a strong interest in the viability of the program and a great sensitivity about it. The issue of board involvement in the athletic program is further complicated by the fact that, as Kerr and Gade observe, "Drawing the lines between what a board does and what the president and other administrators do is a delicate and often controversial matter—what is 'policy' to one person is 'administration' to another and vice versa."[11] Consequently, it is very important for the CEO to keep the board informed about relevant aspects of the athletic program, including philosophic issues pertinent to reform, policies and procedures designed to assure compliance with NCAA legislation, and major changes in that legislation, especially prohibitions against involvement of alumni and friends in an institution's program.

NCAA legislation should be revised to require submission each year, along with the CEO's compliance certification form, of a copy of formal affirmation by the governing board of its commitment for compliance and its assurance that it has assigned responsibility for this to the CEO and has delegated to him or her the full authority for achieving compliance. That formal affirmation should be renewed at not more than five-year intervals. This would clarify for all constituencies of the institution the respective roles of governing board and CEO in the control of abuses in intercollegiate athletics.

The Association of Governing Boards of Universities and Colleges is increasing its activity in helping inform governing-board members about intercollegiate athletics, their responsibilities for this phase of institutional program and the proper roles for discharging those responsibilities. One such effort is the AGB special report prepared by L. Jay Oliva, chancellor of New York University: *What Trustees Should Know About Intercollegiate Athletics.*[12] This very informative document should be studied carefully by all governing board members.

THE ROLE OF THE FACULTY

The quintessential responsibility of a faculty is to ensure the integrity of the institution's academic program. The diagnostic findings set forth in the preceding chapter provide illumination for ways in which the faculty can help prevent the erosion of academic credibility of the institution through its failure to provide a meaningful education for many of its athletes, especially in the sports of football and basketball.

The retreat from academic standards, the widening fissure between the educational mission and the athletic subculture, and the increasing recognition that athletics is the only thing important enough to society to really exempt one from many of the requirements of the university have combined to produce an environment in which it has been easy for many faculty members to accept the athletic program as a necessary evil and one best left in the care of administrators. This lack of enthusiasm by faculty to be a major participant in the governance of intercollegiate athletics can be attributed in part to the loose structure for decision-making in higher education, as noted earlier, and to the higher priority faculty place, indeed are forced to place, on their primary roles in the teaching and research functions of the institution.

> *There are two fundamental problems in bringing the faculty into this arena, one in which they have such a stake. They have a natural inclination not to join with the administration and even though they enjoy the titillation of the initial encounter of these kinds of issues they would rather be at their laboratory desk or in the library or working with students than dealing with these kinds of issues on a continuing basis and with the follow-up that is required to make something happen.*

Because ultimate responsibility for the virtues of honesty and integrity in the institution's educational program rests primarily with the faculty, it is imperative that university faculties become more actively involved as a partner in determining the policies for the conduct of intercollegiate athletics. Like CEOs, they can no longer avoid blame for wrongs done simply by not knowing. The faculty can best discharge its responsibility in the governance of intercollegiate athletics through three representations: faculty senate (council), faculty representative for athletics, and athletic board (committee). The athletic director should be a member of the faculty senate for the same reason he or she should be a member of the academic council—as an official of the institution with primary responsibility for education.

The faculty senate should have a voice in the development and revision of the institution's position on athletics which, as discussed above, should contain all basic policies for the operation of the athletic program. The senate should receive a report at least once each academic year on the athletic program. This should include detailed information about the academic performance of student-athletes and academic support services for them, together with the general features of the monitoring program. There should be continuing open communication between the CEO and faculty senate officers about questions or concerns that arise about the athletic program. This was expressed well by one CEO in advice for his colleagues:

Involve the political machinery of the faculty senate; tell them what the risks are; tell them what the public reaction is likely to be and lay it on the line so they know that their integrity as a faculty is at stake.

In order to achieve meaningful communication with and involvement of the faculty, there must be more open sharing of information. The American Association of University Professors (AAUP) Special Committee on Athletics is correct in its observation that in the past the governance of athletics has been made more difficult because information about the athletic program has been treated as highly secret. As the committee emphasizes, such secretiveness is untenable in the intellectual environment of the academic community, which should be committed to fostering open and candid discussion. And it is antithetical to the effective governance of a program that is, at the same time, so visible and so crucial to the academic and ethical credibility of the university.[13]

The faculty representative for athletics has a critical role to play in the oversight and coordination of the institution's athletic program.[14]

The CEO must have a faculty chairman who can speak to and for the faculty, even though most of the people on the faculty frankly don't care and don't want to be bothered except they want to know that somebody is in control and the institution is not going to be embarrassed and that it is going to be competitive. . . . Be sure you have a faculty chairman and faculty representation on the board who just by their presence give a sense of certainty to the rest of the faculty.

The specific responsibilities of the faculty representative for athletics vary from symbolic functions to the focal role for eligibility certification and compliance monitoring, depending on institutional and conference policies and procedures. In some institutions, the faculty representative is only a shadow figure. In most institutions with major programs, the responsibilities are quite comprehensive and demanding, making it very difficult for one who has not achieved tenured professorial rank to devote the necessary time and energy to the assignment. In those institutions in which the faculty representative plays a key role in athletic program governance the duties are so demanding that released time and secretarial assistance are essential.

THE ROLE OF THE ATHLETIC BOARD

A board in control of athletics or an athletic advisory board (council or committee) is not required by the NCAA. However, if such an entity exists, as it does in most institutions with big-time sports programs, a majority of its members must be faculty or administrators. Most athletic boards are advisory to the president and function much like other university committees. However, a limited number of institutions have autonomous legal corporations, established under state law or institutional policy, for the administration of the athletic program.

Whether operating within the university structure as an advisory body, or functioning as a decision-making entity legally separate from the university, the responsibilities of the athletic board for the control of abuses are the same in principle, but they are discharged in ways that are strikingly different. Responsibility for financial management of the athletic program can logically by transferred to an autonomous board, with appropriate budgetary controls by the president, but the responsibility for academic credibility cannot be delegated to an outside entity. There is, therefore, an inherent danger in this separation when an institution has an autonomous athletic board. Unless appropriate structures and procedures are established to effect the requisite interface with the processes for academic governance of the institution, the fissure between education and athletics can easily broaden.

Regardless of the organizational structure, the role, responsibilities, and procedure for the athletic board must be set forth explicitly in the institution's position on the athletic program, and the board and all related committees must have ready access to all information needed to fulfill their responsibilities in supporting the CEO and in assuring the faculty that every effort is being made to maintain credibility, academic and ethical, in the athletic program.

The members of the athletic committee must assiduously avoid the perception that they have been co-opted by the perquisites traditionally provided those holding these positions: complimentary tickets and preferential seating for athletic events and travel to post-season competition (e.g., bowl games and tournaments). Any such benefits must be for work done to maintain institutional and program integrity and not for favors rendered to help athletic teams win more contests. It is obvious, therefore, that faculty selected for these positions must have the respect and confidence of their faculty colleagues, and they must take seriously the very important assignment given them.

> One of the concerns I have is that over the country, because CEOs are too busy to give minute supervision to all the things that they have to do, we've had athletic councils spring up; and sometimes those athletic councils, which are there to be watchdogs and provide safeguards have become a little too tame and a little too close to the scene. Busy, harried presidents may be tempted to draw too much comfort from the existence of the athletic council.

THE ROLE OF THE ATHLETIC DIRECTOR

How you achieve compliance is really very simple; it's not complex. The thing you must have is key administrators, first, in central administration and, second, within athletics, who understand the centrality of education in the mission of higher education and who have strong ethical values. If you have that, it will work.

An institution has to show its willingness to focus directly on the athletic administration in case you have a problem.

While the CEO is the official ultimately responsible for control of an institution's athletic program, it is the athletic director on whom day-to-day responsibility for that control must rest. The explicit assignment of responsibility and delegation of authority for control is necessary, and this should be clearly understood by all athletic personnel. That this authority truly has been delegated in the institution's chain of command is best communicated by the selection and appointment of the athletic director by the CEO and, in turn, by the fact that the athletic director is responsible for the selection of head coaches.

The CEO does not hire the football coach or basketball coach or any other coach. That's the responsibility of the athletic director. The athletic director makes a recommendation to the president and then the president says yes or no, but we want it very clear to all our coaches, they don't report to the president; they report to the athletic director.

It is the responsibility of the athletic director to administer the intercollegiate program in compliance with all institutional, conference (where applicable), and NCAA policies and regulations, and to do so in ways that promote adherence to basic ethical values and enhancement of education of student-athletes. This is no small task. A successful athletic director needs a broad range of talents and experience, including: technical expertise in sports; experience in marketing, promotion, and fund-raising; and management skills—for human, financial, and physical resources. "Finally and perhaps most importantly," says one who holds that position, "a qualified director of athletics must be an educator."[15] Like the CEO, the athletic director must have courage and must be willing to put his or her job on the line if necessary to maintain integrity for the institution and its program.

In order to fulfill these responsibilities, the athletic director must be actively involved in the development of the institution's position for its athletic programs. Networking of athletic directors in their national organizations, and especially in their respective NCAA division (and subdivision), is important in helping form the horizontal and vertical matrix of institutional representatives necessary to achieve consensus on those issues vital to the environment conducive to reform of college sports.

To help integrate athletics and education, the athletic director should serve on the academic council with deans of colleges and the chief academic officer (academic vice-president or provost). This positions the athletic director to be creative and aggressive in identifying and implementing formal and informal programs that promote integration of athletics and education and that enhance the quality of education, not only for individual student-athletes but for all students. One such program recommended by Richard Lapchick and John Slaughter[16] is the organization of "faculty-coach-athletic department communication forums to discuss the views of each in the contexts of their work." There is a critical need for a variety of activities of this type to help enhance communication between faculty and athletic-department personnel, and athletic directors can be the most effective facilitators for these.

The athletic director must not only be committed to rules compliance, he or she must promote an environment conducive to sensitivity to compliance and must establish the necessary policies and procedures to achieve this. The critical attribute in achieving and maintaining such an environment is attitude. Coaches and other athletic-department staff members must be helped, by education and example, to understand that the monitoring program discussed earlier is designed to help the athletic program succeed by preventing problems. When there is such an understanding and perception, the monitoring program will be characterized by a spirit of cooperation. If, however, the athletic director views the monitoring program as an intrusion that encroaches on his or her prerogatives as the program administrator, this perception will inevitably affect the attitudes of other staff members, who will then view activities designed to help achieve preventive control as police tactics demonstrative of lack of trust or a desire for punitive constraints.

In an environment of understanding and cooperation, the athletic director can organize the various activities that are necessary to promote compliance and to enhance the welfare of student-athletes. These should include but not be limited to:

- Orientation programs for student-athletes dealing with campus life, academic policies and procedures, academic support and other student counseling services, conference and NCAA rules and regulations, and athletic policies and procedures
- Orientation programs for coaches and other staff members for review of institutional, conference, and NCAA regulations
- Policies and procedures for eligibility certification, with emphasis on the absolute necessity for coaches in all sports to comply strictly with

these, and the assignment of responsibility for appropriate checks and balances to avoid inadvertent mistakes resulting in the competition of ineligible players

- Formal process for review and evaluation of the athletic program relative to the institution's position for it, with emphasis on ways to achieve more common areas of interest between athletics and academics

One of the most important tasks of the athletic director is to establish equity within intercollegiate athletics by eradicating discrimination and providing women and minorities with proper opportunities as student-athletes, coaches, and administrators.[17] If both men's and women's programs are administered in the same department under a male athletic director, it is imperative that there be a senior woman administrator responsible for the administration of the women's program and that this person report directly to the athletic director. Failure to do this sends a very strong message—not only to the women student-athletes but also to the student body and the general public—that the department, indeed the institution, is not fully committed to providing equal opportunity for women in its athletic program.

It is highly inappropriate for the position of athletic director to be held by a head coach. This is especially true in institutions with big-time sports programs where such dual responsibility, when it occurs, typically involves the football or basketball coach. Each of these positions is clearly a full-time job, requiring all the time and energies of the incumbent if it is done properly. In the context of abuse control, furthermore, the most compelling reason for such segregation of responsibility is the fact that there is inherently a conflict of interest—or the inevitable appearance of one, which must be avoided as assiduously as if it were reality—when the head coach is responsible, as athletic director, for policing his or her own program and for resource allocation for other sports.

THE ROLE OF THE COACH

As noted earlier, effective control of an endemic disease requires team effort, with wise policies and a well-designed strategic plan developed at the top and communicated, with unwavering commitment, to the field forces for implementation. In the application of this medical analogy to the control of abuses in college sports, coaches are the workers on whom the success of the campaign largely will depend. Consequently, much is expected of them; indeed, must be required of them. Because the stakes are so high for all concerned, coaches are entitled to be well informed and well supported.

Consistent with the principle of transfer of responsibility and authority discussed thus far, the head coach of a sport is directly responsible for the operation of that entire program. As one well-known football coach in Division I-A has observed, when the president of the institution "clearly defines what the aims and objectives are in regard to the athletic program, the coach knows immediately where he or she stands. When the president, athletic director, and coach work closely together, serious problems should not exist."[18]

The institutional position for its athletic program must clearly establish the role of the coach as a teacher, not merely for the enhancement of athletic ability but also for the responsibility for promoting and contributing to the total education of the student-athlete in his or her program. The role of coaches as educators, neglected in the past, should receive much attention as efforts are made to span the fissure that now exists between athletics and academics. The potential contribution coaches can make to education is suggested in this observation by a prominent head football coach in Division I-A: "If the coach is not convinced that education is important to that student-athlete, the student-athlete is not going to be interested in going to class and making as good grades as he can. He's got the only excuse he needs. The man he looks up to for all his guidance has made it clear that it really doesn't matter what he does as long as he shows up on Saturday and gets it in the end zone. He's been taught from day one: you please the coach and everything's OK."

In order to fulfill such an awesome responsibility, coaches need to remain on campus far more than is currently the case. More will be said about this in the discussion of recruiting (in chapter 4), one of the major issues that must be addressed through cooperative effort on a national basis if there is to be meaningful reform of college sports. In the evaluation of the coach's performance, "winning" must be redefined to include achieving success in a proper balance of education and athletics. It is in this type determination that the faculty should play a definitive role.

While the coach must be held responsible for promoting successful academic performance of student-athletes, requiring a specific graduation rate, as suggested by some, is questionable. Student-athletes should, of course, be strongly encouraged to perform well academically and should be provided the necessary assistance to do so. However, the individual student-athlete is the one, in the final analysis, who is responsible for learning, and it is inappropriate to hold anyone else responsible for the failure of the individual to do so when appropriate encouragement is given and a proper environment is provided.

In addition to the responsibility for promoting the total education and enhancing the welfare of student-athletes in their programs, the coach shares another major responsibility—adherence to the basic values of ethical behavior. The value system of the head coach will be a major factor in determining the behavior of the assistant coaches and student-athletes in compliance with regulations governing conduct, both on and off the playing field. The ideal model is seen in the football coach (in Division I-A) who, a few years ago, was becoming uneasy because he felt that pressures were building up for actions he was unwilling to take, with the result that he probably would begin to lose ball games because of his refusal to do those things. He said to a friend, "The day that I am pressured or forced to engage in unethical behavior in order to win, I won't coach anymore." That coach is today one of the nation's most successful and respected. Fortunately, there are many like him. Still, many others are willing not merely to bend, but to break, the rules in order to achieve their goal—winning.

In his discussion of the responsibility of coaches in the ethical conduct of college sports, the football coach who commented above on the interrelationship of president, athletic director, and coach refers to the code of ethics approved in 1952 by the American Football Coaches' Association:

> The distinguishing characteristic of a profession is that its members are dedicated to rendering a service to humanity. Personal gain must be of lesser consideration. Those who select football coaching must understand the justification for football is that it provides spiritual and physical values for those who play it, and the game belongs, essentially, to the players.
>
> The welfare of the game depends on how the coaches live up to the spirit and letter of ethical conduct and how coaches remain ever mindful of the high trust and confidence placed in them by their players and by the public.
>
> Coaches unwilling or unable to comply with the principles of the Code of Ethics have no place in the profession.

He affirms, "This code is easy for coaches to understand and should not be that difficult to follow."[19] Easy to understand: yes. Easy to follow: not in contemporary society. Therein lies the challenge for higher education and for each institution. Coaches' organizations must also recognize their responsibility for policing themselves in controlling unethical conduct if coaches are to fulfill the responsibilities of their position.

The education necessary to instill in coaches an understanding of and respect for the centrality of education in the institution's mission and a recognition of the importance of ethical behavior requires continuing and intensive effort. As previously noted, new members of the athletic fraternity are often socialized into occupationally related, role-specific deviant ethical behavior. This behavior contributes to achieving organizational goals and objectives such as winning. Therefore it is incumbent on institutions, conferences, and national organizations—not only the NCAA but others, especially coaches' organizations—to identify and implement ways to instill understanding of and respect for these values.

Recent changes in NCAA legislation and the association's enforcement practices should help deter unethical behavior. Now penalties for serious violations must follow the coach who moves to another institution, and a coach (or other athletic staff) found guilty of a violation and who at that time is no longer active in athletics at a member institution may be required to come before the Infractions Committee before becoming employed in athletics at a member institution during a specified time period (up to twelve years in a recent case) to determine whether NCAA penalties should be imposed that would limit his or her duties at that institution. The time during which penalties follow a coach moving to another institution should be extended from the current provision of two years, and institutions should not limit the time for punitive action on such coaches to the minimum period required by NCAA legislation.

Perhaps of greatest importance in this context is the unequivocal position established by the CEO, as illustrated in the example referenced earlier in which the CEO personally informs all athletic staff annually, orally and in writing, that anyone found to have intentionally violated NCAA rules will be fired. This penalty should be imposed on coaches for violations not only at the institution where currently employed, but also for others at institutions where the coach had been previously employed.

Even though the specter of punishment is necessary and should serve as a deterrent, it is only a partial solution. A far more effective approach is to address the issue of pressures upon a coach to win, and these are much more complex than generally recognized. Considerable evidence indicates that the pressure to win is due more to self-imposed goals than to external forces. These goals are the function of such qualities as one's innate desire to win (to achieve the greatest level of performance of which one is capable), egocentricity, the desire for prestige or economic rewards, or ambition to move up to a larger program.

> *In plain fact I think that in Division I-A most of the cheating is done by coaches who want to win for the security of their job only because the job provides most of the things their ego wants: money, influence, recognition, power—all those things. To say all these people have to cheat because they are pressured by the institution, the president, the AD, the fans or somebody —that's a cop-out. . . . A lot of them cheat because they want to win themselves no matter what else; they want what goes with winning. . . . The pressure is self-generated.*

This observation by a CEO in Division I-A, previously quoted in chapter 2, was reinforced by a CEO in a Division III institution who commented:

> *I am also concerned because I see a lot of people affected by the whole Division I notion. We have young coaches coming in now, and they don't have a Division III mentality. They are starting here, but they want to be up there in Division I in a few years.*

Colleagues in both Divisions II and III expressed the view that such ambitions make many individuals more likely to succumb to the temptation to win because they look upon winning as *the* way to achieve upward mobility in coaching.

In recent years, the suggestion has often been made that, in order to reduce the pressures to win, head coaches should be given academic tenure. Historically, the reason for granting tenure has been to assure academic freedom for faculty in the pursuit and transmission of knowledge. Therefore, tenure is not appropriate as a mechanism for job security for coaches. A contract for a specified term, with mutually agreed-upon conditions for extension, is the more appropriate arrangement, and the contract should include explicit criteria for evaluation of performance. As emphasized earlier, these criteria should include not merely the won-lost record, but also the effectiveness of the coach in promoting academic success and ethical conduct of team members. With respect to the question of appropriateness of tenure as job security for a coach, it should be remembered that even university presidents do not have tenure in their positions as chief executive officers. Instead, they characteristically are subject to annual evaluation and to renewal or not at the pleasure of the governing board.

THE ROLE OF STUDENT-ATHLETES AND RESPONSIBILITY FOR STUDENT-ATHLETE WELFARE

A full athletic scholarship ought to represent an opportunity to get a good education. That is a commodity of immense value.

As I see intercollegiate athletics, the more serious problems of sickness are in the exploitation of youngsters. . . . The educational process is here after all for youngsters. . . . And sickness in its present form is where we send youngsters out who can no longer do the only thing that's been important in their life since middle school and they have no skills to do anything else—that is what is endemic in the system we have today.

Universities should be among the first to reaffirm the importance of basic values, such as honesty, promise keeping, free expression, and nonviolence, for these are not only principles essential to civilized society; they are values on which all learning and discovery ultimately depend.[20]

There are no more important benefits of college sports than those which accrue to the active participants—the student-athletes. They therefore have a major role to play in controlling abuses in order for these benefits to continue for generations of students who follow them. While the institution and many individuals share in the responsibility for providing the proper environment for learning, as will be discussed later, it is the student-athlete who is ultimately responsible for his or her education. The importance of education in preparation for a meaningful life when the roar of the crowd is only a memory is strikingly clear from the estimates on the number of high-school student-athletes who make the football and basketball teams of NCAA member institutions, progress to senior status in college, and then make the cut for professional teams:

TABLE 3.1 Estimates of High-School Participants in Football and Men's Basketball Who Achieve College and Professional Status

STATUS	FOOTBALL	BASKETBALL
Number High-School Senior Participants	265,000	150,000
Number Making Teams of NCAA Institutions (Freshmen)	16,450	3,800
Number Playing as Seniors	8,930	2,400
Number Making Cut, Professional Teams	215	64

(Source: *NCAA News*, October 9, 1989)

The average professional career is less than five years, and most of those with the shorter stints are not financially secure and are at a great disadvantage if their education has not prepared them for life beyond the university. The efforts of many elements of society must be galvanized to help young students recognize that a quality education, not athletics, is the route that offers the greatest opportunity for upward social and economic mobility, for a meaningful and productive life. This was the message communicated to blue-chip recruits at a banquet in Birmingham, Alabama, in January 1990 by Tony Dorset, former Heisman Trophy winner and ten-year veteran in the NFL:

> If I had it to do over again I'd go back and apply myself a little more academically. I have friends who are pro athletes who can't even write a check, or they have to have their wives balance the checkbook. That's sad. I know guys who've gone through the education system and still can't read. You better get a quality education while you can because when it is all over that's what you will have to depend on.[21]

Student-athletes have an obligation to respect the basic values of ethical behavior. This is particularly true with regard to the rules of the game—not just the rules governing the competition in various sports but also the larger body of rules adopted for the conduct of intercollegiate athletics.

As a condition of eligibility each student-athlete must sign, before the first competition in each academic year, a statement affirming that he or she has had the more significant NCAA regulations affecting eligibility reviewed by the athletic director (or his or her representative) and that the student-athlete is not in violation of those regulations. There are few more brazen examples of dishonesty than to have an intelligent student-athlete make such affirmation annually for four years after having accepted, for example, an expensive sports car and a considerable sum of money in return for agreeing to go to a given institution, having accepted monthly payments while there, and then, after becoming a wealthy professional athlete, to publicize ostentatiously the hypocrisy and wrongdoing of the institution for all the recruiting inducements and extra benefits given him by coaches or representatives of the institution's athletic interest.

The responsibility of student-athletes for ethical conduct is a subject on which greater emphasis must be placed in order to achieve effective control of college sports. Our failure to have given this the attention needed in recent years is probably due, at least in part, to the traditional view that moral training is the responsibility primarily of the family, religious institutions, and early childhood education, and that the foundation determining one's pattern of ethical conduct is established long before college age is reached. There is much validity to this view, but colleges and universities can no longer continue to neglect their responsibility for helping overcome deficiencies that may exist in students entering their portals. Programs designed specifically for student-athletes on moral reasoning and ethical behavior must be a high priority for each institution and for conferences, and the NCAA presidents commission should provide leadership in affirming the importance of such programs and in promoting their development and implementation. An increasing number of institutions are initiating programs to assist undergraduates in clarifying the values by which they live.[22] Programs of this type can be designed to address specific problems faced by student-athletes.

The fact that student-athletes from lower socioeconomic backgrounds have been found to be less likely to recognize the moral legitimacy of the NCAA's amateurism regulations,[23] and that many student-athletes may actually think they are not doing anything wrong when they accept money (or merchandise) from alumni or others, does not relieve colleges and universities of the responsibility for instructing these students about moral reasoning and ethical behavior. Indeed, it underscores the importance of their doing so.

The NCAA constitution specifies that "intercollegiate athletics programs shall be conducted in a manner designed to protect and enhance the physical and educational welfare of student-athletes." The results of the research conducted for the NCAA in 1987-1988 academic year show clearly that too many institutions have failed to adhere to this principle.[24] Formal responsibility for the welfare of student-athletes begins with their enrollment, but sensitivity to it should affect their recruitment. Furthermore, colleges and universities should provide the leadership, set the standards, and send an unequivocal message to youngsters, their parents, their teachers, and their coaches that athletic ability alone will not guarantee a positive response from the director of admissions, even though enrollment of a student is desired by the coach, and that it certainly will not permit a student-athlete to maintain eligibility for four seasons. As noted earlier, the NCAA membership has made a little progress on the matter of academic standards by the adoption and implementation of freshman eligibility and satisfactory-progress requirements. The fact remains, however, that current requirements are too low for most institutions, based on the standards to which nonathlete students are held. Consequently, institutions must resist pressures to admit students who do not have a reasonable chance of success academically, regardless of their athletic abilities.

While it is certainly inappropriate for the NCAA to attempt to legislate on every detail of optimum academic standards for its member institutions in various divisions, it is essential that reasonable minimum standards in certain areas be adopted. Such requirements should permit institutions in respective divisions to build upon individual standards that are in keeping with institutional philosophies while at the same time permitting their athletic programs to remain sufficiently competitive to survive. Therefore, as soon as sufficient data are available from the current NCAA academic research project to which reference has been made, consideration should be given to strengthening the freshman eligibility requirements, with particular attention to an equitable indexing to eliminate the rigidity of the fixed cut-off score on the college-entrance examination.

The often-expressed criticism that current academic eligibility requirements in Division I result in denial of access to higher education is not valid and should not be accepted as justification for admitting inadequately prepared student-athletes to four-year colleges and universities, particularly the nation's research universities. The point has been made that such changes in Proposition 48 as elimination of partial qualifiers would not deny opportunities for access mostly to black students because Division I institutions would award "virtually the same number of athletic scholarships to black athletes as before, but those who get them, while slightly poorer athletes, will be better and more motivated students who are far more likely to get a meaningful college education that will equip them to live successful and productive adult lives."[25] Its diversity is one of the great strengths of American higher education, and that diversity provides opportunity for access for students with different levels of academic preparation. For universities to disregard this is to show lack of commitment to the central mission of higher education and to subvert that in order to provide entertainment for the public— entertainment of a type that can be provided by other entities. Two-year colleges provide access to postsecondary education for students who, for a variety of reasons, including inadequate academic preparation and personal preference, are not ready to perform successfully in more rigorous four-year college programs. Enrollment in such institutions provides the option to continue in four-year institutions.

The prediction that the failure to admit the most highly skilled athletes to the institutions with big-time sports programs would result in a decline in enthusiasm and support for their athletic programs because of the diminished entertainment value of those programs demonstrates, we believe, a lack of understanding and appreciation of the true essence of the appeal of college sports to an institution's several major constituencies. With appropriate regulations for minimal academic standards to assure reasonable equity of competition, a slight reduction in level of skill on the part of participants will not affect appreciably the enthusiasm, excitement, and loyalty of students, alumni, and other fans who find enjoyment in, and achieve a sense of community from, college sports. The "quality of the product" argument is relevant only when college sports are judged as mass entertainment in direct competition with professional sports, not as an integral part of quality higher education.

I think these youngsters will meet the challenge, meet the standards. But on the other hand, if all of us are about the same in our standards, the general public is not going to recognize the difference in quality. It is still going to be just as exciting. And I think we are ultimately going to use as a carrot a powerful incentive for a segment of our population to perform better in high school.

Once the decision is made and the student-athlete enrolls in an institution, the responsibilities for an environment that protects and enhances student-athlete welfare increase in number and importance. Among the features of that environment are the following:

- Effective communication about institutional, conference, and NCAA policies and regulations
- Appropriate and adequate academic support service
- Opportunities for social development as well as academic achievement
- Protection and enhancement of physical welfare
- Emphasis on respect for basic values of ethical behavior

It is apparent that to fulfill these responsibilities institutions must treat student-athletes differently from others in the general student body in certain activities of college life. While this is contrary to a fundamental principle on which much NCAA legislation is based (i.e., that student-athletes must be treated in the same way as other students) and also runs counter to humane concerns of educational institutions, it is indeed necessary in certain areas and can be justified by the unique nature of intercollegiate athletics. Institutions must always be very sensitive to the tensions involved, both in the academic community and in the view of the general public, as difficult decisions are made on the proper course of action in individual cases warranting differential treatment.

The importance of effective communication with student-athletes on a continuing basis cannot be overemphasized. This must include in-depth orientations about all aspects of academic and social campus life and should be reinforced by comprehensive student-athlete handbooks that are reviewed and updated annually. To demonstrate institutional concern for the academic and social development of the student-athlete, ranking officials from units of central administration and academic programs should participate in the orientation sessions and do so in a meaningful way—not merely make a courtesy, perfunctory appearance. It must be remembered that communication involves more than oral or written messages. As expressed by A. Bartlett Giamatti, an educational institution teaches far more, and more profoundly, by how it acts than by anything anyone within it ever says.[26] It is not sufficient, for example, to simply say during the orientation session and in meetings thereafter that academic performance, and therefore class attendance, are important. Actions must be taken on a continuing basis to demonstrate that this is truly a commitment, not merely a position to which lip service is given.

Because of the demands on their time and energy for practice and competition (including travel for the latter), and the fact that some of them are less well prepared academically than the general student body,[27] student-athletes should have access to not only the full range of counseling services provided for all students, but also to additional academic-support services needed to help them be successful in the classroom as well as on the playing field or court. That academic-support program should supplement, not replace, the academic counseling provided by the academic unit in which the student-athlete is enrolled. In those institutions with big-time sports programs, academic-support services for student-athletes are generally funded by the athletic department, and this is only proper. Increasingly, the administration of these programs is being made a function of the office of academic affairs. In some institutions this may be necessary in order to correct grave flaws in the program and to achieve credibility for it. In keeping with the central concept of this treatise—the necessity for integration of athletics and education—decisions about the administrative responsibility for, and physical location of, the academic-support program, as well as its regular monitoring and evaluation, should be examined carefully by each institution. For reasons given earlier, this is another activity in which the faculty should have a seminal role. The goal must be to design and implement a program that reduces the dysfunctional impact of athletics on the education of student-athletes and that is perceived as having integrity because the athletic community is fulfilling its responsibilities.

Social development and the acquisition of personal skills necessary for successful living are as much a part of a quality college education as the acquisition of knowledge in the classroom or laboratory. This is an area to which institutions need to give much more attention and in which more program activities should be planned to assist student-athletes, often in cooperation with members of the academic faculty. To promote social development of student-athletes, consideration should be given to the elimination of athletic dormitories, as recommended by Richard Schultz.[28]

In considering the responsibility of student-athletes and others for their successful academic performance, we do well to note again the finding from the 1987-1988 National Study of Intercollegiate Athletics that football and basketball players reported many more problems with extreme tiredness or exhaustion than student-athletes in other sports. It is not surprising, therefore, that these student-athletes "report that it is harder to make their academic work their top priority and to get the grades they are capable of getting." The importance of this point is underscored in this study by student responses to the questions: "Are there things about your life at college you would like to tell us that we did not ask you? If so, what are they?" Some of the comments about health status and satisfaction with health care related to concerns about injuries or medical care but: "many more comments, however, concerned fatigue and exhaustion due to being a student-athlete."[29]

Maintaining good physical condition and strength year-round is obviously necessary for the welfare of student-athletes, but when football-team members, for example, exert themselves in "voluntary" strength and conditioning programs during the winter (after regular season and before spring practice) to the extent that they are so exhausted when they go to their classes they fall asleep, it is obvious that academic and athletic priorities are not in balance and that the welfare of the student-athlete is being disregarded. The point must be made again: when a student-athlete is required to reach his or her highest possible level of athletic achievement without regard to whether the individual has time or energy to meet only minimal academic requirements to maintain eligibility, the institution is demonstrating a lack of regard not only for the welfare of student-athletes but also for the centrality of education in its mission. That will inevitably have an impact on student-athletes who desire to achieve a balance between athletics and education and ultimately on nonathlete students and other constituencies of the university. The NCAA must establish limits on the time that can be devoted to competition, practice, and conditioning programs; these should be tailored to the needs of each sport. It must be remembered, also, that limiting the time to these activities will not, of itself, assure that student-athletes will use that time for enhancing the quality of their education.[30]

Several points about the physical welfare of student-athletes merit consideration. In the 1987-1988 National Study of Intercollegiate Athletes it was found that student-athletes generally report themselves more satisfied with the medical care they receive from their institutions than were the nonathlete students engaged in other extracurricular activities. Any indication that they were less satisfied than the comparison group would have been both surprising and disappointing, for NCAA regulations permit institutions to provide the full cost of medical care resulting from illness or injury directly related to participation (practice or competition) in intercollegiate athletics. Indeed, institutions recognize that as an obligation, and most certainly strive to fulfill their responsibilities for quality medical care.

The matter of long-term disability insurance for student-athletes injured during practice or competition is one which should have more careful study. The NCAA has demonstrated concern and has taken leadership in this area and currently pays (from the revenues from the Division I men's basketball tournament) the premium for catastrophic athletic injury insurance for men's and women's basketball-team members in Division I. In doing so, it has made it possible for the rates for student-athletes in other sports (in all divisions) to be reduced. The percentages of participating institutions in the NCAA lifetime catastrophic athletic injury insurance program in fiscal year 1988-1989 were as follows: Division I: 73 percent, Division II: 48 percent and Division III: 45 percent. (See our recommendation on this matter in the section titled "NCAA Structure and Distribution of Revenue" in chapter 4.)

The physical welfare of student athletes goes far beyond medical care while in college or insurance against disability from athletic injury. One of the more important areas in which both the student-athlete and the institution have shared responsibilities is that of substance abuse, including the use of tobacco products, alcohol, and other drugs. Fortunately, national education programs on the harmful effects of tobacco have had a very positive influence in reducing the percentage of Americans in all age groups who smoke. This change in behavior occurred only after there was a change in attitude about the harmful effects of tobacco. The one area in which the reduction in use of tobacco has been less marked is in the use of smokeless tobacco products. The sport in which this is perhaps of most importance is baseball, in which players and coaches have traditionally had a high frequency of use of smokeless tobacco products. Coaches have an obligation to promote abstinence from all tobacco products in view of the definitive evidence of their adverse effects on health.

Institutions should be mindful of their responsibilities to help deter the use of alcoholic beverages by student-athletes, indeed by all students, in view of the widespread evidence that alcohol consumption is the most serious problem related to personal injury and civil disorder of college students. The fact that alcohol is an illegal drug for individuals under twenty-one years of age makes the matter of institutional responsibility more sensitive and complex.[31]

Institutions, conferences, and the NCAA should consider carefully the following recommendations of the *White House Conference for a Drug Free America* in planning programs to enhance student-athlete welfare and in their use of advertising of alcoholic beverages for revenue to support their sports programs:

- Athletes at all levels must make a personal commitment to remain drug-free.
- Organized sports institutions should design and implement comprehensive antidrug policies.
- Sports organizations, amateur and professional, should ensure that their activities and their members do not promote, endorse, or condone the illegal consumption of alcohol or the abuse of alcohol.
- Concrete actions must be taken immediately to discourage all young people from using alcohol and tobacco. These actions should include clear and consistent "no use" messages concerning alcohol and tobacco, content and warning labels on alcoholic beverages, stronger enforcement of purchase and public-possession-of-alcohol laws for minors, and restriction of alcohol and tobacco advertising according to existing industry guidelines.[32]

In spite of the widely publicized unequivocal evidence of the damage to mind and body of illicit drugs, the plague of substance abuse continues to be one of the greatest perils, and seemingly intractable problems, faced by our society. Available evidence indicates that substance abuse by student-athletes is not higher than by nonathlete students or by the college-age population generally. Unfortunately, the publicity given the instances of substance abuse by student-athletes contributes to the perception that a higher percentage of them do engage in substance abuse.

The importance of a strong, healthy body should be the most effective motivation for student-athletes to resist the temptation of substance abuse and should, accordingly, be a strong argument for institutions to help student-athletes recognize their responsibility to resist that temptation. Aside from health enhancement, student-athletes have a heavy responsibility for avoiding use of drugs that have the potential for performance enhancement—a responsibility stimulated by regard for values of ethical behavior. Taking performance-enhancing drugs is a decision to cheat! As one CEO observed,

In our incredible enthusiasm for athletics, we expect to see records broken every year. We admire that achievement in competitive sports so much. From that human instinct arises the temptation to excess —if we admire perfection, then if we take anabolic steroids, maybe we'll be even

better than we've been before. Since we like winning, it's easy to do things conducive to winning that may not be ethical. . . . We need to understand the temptation to excess, and we need to combat it.

These two reasons—better health and welfare of the student-athlete and assurance of competitive equity—have been the motivation for the NCAA drug-testing and drug-education programs, and for similar programs adopted by conferences and individual institutions. Much anecdotal evidence indicates that these programs are having a strong deterrent effect. Institutions and student-athletes have an obligation to work together to fulfill their respective responsibilities for deterring substance abuse. In this context, it is imperative that institutions help student-athletes understand more clearly the responsibility they have for helping students of high-school age, and younger, to avoid substance abuse. As athletes, they are role models, regardless of whether that is their desire or intent. Helping student-athletes to recognize the fact that they are role models in these areas, and helping them in finding ways to serve as effective role models, may indeed be one of the best ways that colleges and universities can promote enhancement of education in these areas so critical for our society.

Helpful as formal institutional programs may be, nothing is more important in helping student-athletes develop an understanding of and respect for basic values than the examples set for them by the ethical conduct of their coaches and, of course, faculty, staff, and other colleagues. This challenge to be models of committed integrity emphasizes as much or more than anything else the necessity for unified commitment and action by the various individuals and groups—horizontal and vertical—in the control of abuses in college sports.

In the planning and implementation of all programs for student-athletes, institutions should have a formal mechanism for securing the involvement of student-athlete advisory committees. Such committees provide benefits at the institutional level, and they also serve as the beginning point for a network, operating through conferences or other regional structures, to provide input for the student-athletes who make up the national committee authorized and established in 1989 by the NCAA in an effort to secure input from student-athletes about NCAA programs and legislation.

Finally, with respect to the responsibility for student-athlete welfare, colleges and universities should not be party to regulations or policies that hold student-athletes hostage and prevent their withdrawing to pursue careers in professional sports before they exhaust their collegiate eligibility. As emphasized by Joe Paterno,[33] student-athletes should be physically and emotionally prepared for the demanding experience of professional football and should be counseled and encouraged to complete their education to be prepared for life after the "roar of the crowd." However, for college officials to support restrictive NFL-draft regulations suggests a greater concern on their part about protecting their investment than sensitivity to the welfare of student-athletes. Such a posture supports the argument of critics who charge that colleges are merely operating a minor league for the NFL.

THE ROLE OF EXTERNAL CONSTITUENCIES

The alumni of an institution constitute the most important external constituency with a role in the control of problems in intercollegiate athletics. That role is critical. Alumni must not involve themselves in any aspect of the athletic program without explicit approval of responsible institutional officials. This is particularly important in matters of recruiting and benefits for student-athletes. They should not only refrain from wrongdoing; they should support fully the efforts of the CEO and other institutional officials to operate a program characterized by ethical conduct and proper balance between athletics and academics.

Most representatives of an institution's athletics interests, as defined in NCAA legislation, are alumni of the institution and most "boosters" are also alumni, but some of the most rabid fans are individuals who have never attended the institution but adopt it because of fervent interest in sports. Consequently, the term "fans" is used here to include not only those who are graduates or former students of an institution, but also those who have a relationship to the institution's athletic program that can make the individuals representatives of its athletics interests.

The fact that fans have been involved in most cases in which an institution has been placed on probation accompanied by other penalties is evidence of the important role they play in the control of problems in college sports. There is perhaps no more striking example than that of an institution on which severe penalties were imposed by the NCAA Committee on Infractions in 1989, an institution on which a major penalty had been imposed only a decade earlier. According to the NCAA news release on the findings in this case, both the institution and the NCAA enforcement staff, in their investigations, found "numerous persons who were willing to give large gifts, pay for cars, provide airline tickets and other benefits upon being approached by assistant coaches. These persons did not seem to be hard to find nor did they hesitate when asked to contribute."

In this case the institution was required to disassociate fourteen representatives of its athletic interests from its athletic program because of their involvement in violations of NCAA rules. It would be difficult to fault the conclusion of the infractions committee in this case that, "It is an atmosphere which must be changed if there is to be a future for the university's athletic program." Sadly, the problem is much deeper. The credibility of an institution's academic program is also in jeopardy if practices of this type continue unchanged. One of the more distressing aspects of such improper involvement of fans in abuses is the fact that frequently they are professionals (e.g., doctors and lawyers) who are guided by a professional code of ethics in their own work and who cannot be excused as uninformed or misguided, but who are wealthy people who take pride in their vicarious involvement with power coaches and successful athletic programs.

The NCAA membership has made many changes in the association's legislation over the past decade to restrict the involvement of fans in athletic programs in an effort to prevent abuses. As late as 1982, an alumnus or friend of the institution could, for example, transport a prospect to the institution's campus for an official visit, provided no family member, relative, or friend was transported and, also, that no food or entertainment was provided en route to or from the campus. In 1983 legislation was changed to prohibit off-campus contacts of prospects (or their relatives or legal guardian) by fans for purpose of athletic recruitment. Consequently, they could no longer transport a prospect to the campus for an official visit. As a further effort to eliminate the involvement of fans in the recruiting of prospects, legislation was changed in 1987 to prohibit all athletic recruiting contacts by fans, on or off the institution's campus, including telephone calls or correspondence.

Two points are important relative to the evolution of these regulations, which are viewed by some as unduly restrictive. First, the prohibition is against contacts for the purpose of athletic recruitment and does not preclude normal civility in interpersonal relationships, either in one's community or on the institution's campus. Second, these changes have had strong support by coaches, who have recognized the necessity for such restrictions in order to *send a message* to alumni and others that they are to refrain from any involvement in recruiting.

Institutions have the responsibility to inform their alumni about pertinent NCAA regulations and the institution's commitment to comply with them, which can be accomplished through alumni publications and club meetings. This and other relevant NCAA legislation affecting alumni as individuals or groups (e.g., prohibition against alumni involvement in the making of community awards to an institution's student-athlete in recognition of athletic achievement) should be brought to the attention of alumni on a recurring basis. This is particularly effective when either the CEO, director of compliance, or official responsible for monitoring the athletic program has a regular column in the general alumni publication or the sports newsletter discussing issues applicable to alumni and friends of the institution. In extreme cases, wealthy alumni with deep involvement in their alma mater's athletic program have vehemently proclaimed that the NCAA could not make them comply with its regulations. In taking such an adversarial position, they overlook the fact that it is the institution that has the responsibility to control its alumni and friends, and if they are unwilling to accept the restraint placed on them by the legislation adopted by the NCAA membership, then it is their alma mater, for which they profess loyalty and support, that must suffer the consequences.

Because of the damage done to institutions by perverse actions of individuals professing loyalty to "their school," some states have begun to enact legislation making it illegal for anyone to provide improper inducements or extra benefits to a student-athlete and providing that an institution can sue to recover damages when such action results in loss of eligibility of a student-athlete and thus causes the institution to lose revenue (e.g., in the form of television, bowl, or tournament revenue). Similar legislation will likely be adopted in other states. That such extreme measures are necessary is evidence of the challenge faced by individual institutions and higher education generally to gain the support of not only alumni but of the general public in addressing the fundamental causes of abuses in intercollegiate athletics.

THE ROLE OF NATIONAL AND REGIONAL ATHLETIC ORGANIZATIONS

While control of intercollegiate athletics can only be achieved at the institutional level, it cannot be achieved under current conditions by an institution acting alone. It is essential that the institution have the help of strong partners, at least at the national level. Most institutions find it desirable to form regional affiliations in the form of conferences for additional assistance. These partnerships are necessary because of the operation of many countervailing forces, perhaps none more important than the need for competitive equity as expressed in one of thirteen principles for the conduct of intercollegiate athletics in the NCAA constitution:

> The structure and programs of the Association and the activities of its members shall promote opportunity for equity in competition to assure that individual student-athletes and institutions will not be prevented unfairly from achieving the benefits inherent in participation in intercollegiate athletics.[34]

This desire for a "level playing field" is so strong that the NCAA membership has expanded greatly the number and specificity of regulations by which they define the parameters for control of their varsity sports programs. Striking evidence of this is seen in the growth of the *NCAA Manual*: from 99 pages in 1967 to 399 in 1989.[35] While striving for the goal of a perfectly level playing field, which can never really be achieved, member institutions must also deal with individuals who feel compelled to cut corners or even to engage in blatant wrongdoing in order to gain a competitive advantage. In such an environment, the national entity establishes the minimal standards (for the entire organization or divisions thereof), and the individual institution determines its more restrictive parameters, consistent with its unique mission and values. The regional entity assists its members in achieving higher compatibility than possible at the national level and also in meeting the requirements of the national entity. Characteristically, the regional entity is an athletic conference that conducts its own championships and has an interface of variable intimacy with the national entity on behalf of the conference membership in the development and implementation of, and compliance with, governing legislation.

NCAA

I firmly believe IAAUS* will finally dominate the collegiate athletic world. It stands for purity, for national control, for fair play. . . . As its aims and methods become better understood, its strength will grow, until its influence will become truly national.

In unity is strength, and all the ills of college athletics would be near solution if every college became an active partisan of this organization.[36]

In these words Palmer Pierce, first president of the NCAA, accurately prophesied, in 1907, the dominating role that the new organization, which then had only forty-nine member institutions, would ultimately have in the college athletic world. Unfortunately, the ills of college athletics have proved to be much more intractable than he envisioned.

The evolution of the role of the NCAA in the control of abuses in college sports has been striking, albeit somewhat spasmodic. In its early years, the association's efforts were directed primarily to game-rules making and to work with game officials, and the principle of "home rule" was followed in the application of legislation enacted by the membership. Evidence of the strong support of this concept was the bylaw provision "specifying that the acceptance of any definite set of eligibility rules is not to be a condition of membership in the NCAA." Even though without regulatory powers at that time, the association in 1922 adopted a ten-point code in which member institutions were urged to, among other things, abide by the association's definition of amateurism, adopt eligibility rules, maintain absolute faculty control of athletics, and organize in regional conferences—presumably for the adoption and enforcement of regulations.[37]

In 1946 the association adopted "Principles for Conduct of Intercollegiate Athletics," known colloquially as the "sanity code" because of the prevailing

---

*For the first few years after its formation in 1906, the organization used the name Intercollegiate Athletic Association of the United States.

belief that adherence to such principles was necessary to restore sanity to the conduct of intercollegiate athletics. These principles were repealed in 1951, and in 1952 legislation was adopted establishing an enforcement program that has evolved into its current form set forth in bylaws 19 and 32 of the *NCAA Manual*.[38]

The regulatory or enforcement function of the NCAA is responsible for most of the frequent, and often harsh, criticism of the organization by the media, the general public, and even representatives of member institutions. Most of the criticism is unjustified and fails to take into account the fact that the NCAA enforcement program, as well as the entire process by which it is implemented, has been mandated by or has the endorsement of the membership for which it is applicable. Regulatory activity, whether instituted by governmental agency or self-imposed by a voluntary organization such as the NCAA, will always evoke discomfort and often criticism from those negatively affected by it. Nevertheless, if the NCAA did not exist, it would be necessary to establish an organization comparable to it for the governance of intercollegiate athletics. The question then is, how can the NCAA be more effective in helping institutions control their athletic programs? Any meaningful answer to this question requires a degree of specificity, because of the diverse functions performed by the NCAA and the range of entities responsible for the processes by which those functions are discharged.

Principles of disease control provide guidance for defining functions of NCAA entities that serve to enhance the ability of institutions to control abuses in their athletic programs. The most important of these principles are: (1) the necessity for accurate diagnosis and correct delineation of causes, and (2) the recognition of the advantages of prevention over corrective intervention. In the application of these principles to the control of abuses in college sports, greater emphasis must be placed on the adoption and implementation of better legislation designed to address the fundamental causes of abuses and to lessen the effects of secondary causes. Much more integration of effort on the part of NCAA staff, committees, council, and presidents commission is required to achieve a better understanding of the causes of abuses, of the effects of alternative approaches for control, and of the value of a holistic approach to control, with emphasis on prevention. Diligent work is required to develop legislation with a minimum of flaws that is based on these principles. Of equal importance, it is necessary that there be both exemplary leadership and intense effort to develop consensus—at the institutional, conference, and national levels—on the rationale and value of proposed legislation.

That progress is being made in these areas is evident. Perhaps the best example is the revision of the legislative calendar (effective for the 1991 convention) to provide adequate time for interaction of the entities mentioned in the development of proposed legislation, not only to reduce its flaws but also to permit involvement of the membership for building stronger consensus. Two points are of utmost importance in planning for the development, adoption, and implementation of legislation to address more effectively abuses in college sports: the complexity of the issues must not be underestimated, and the importance of consensus-building cannot be over-estimated. Experience of the last five years should demonstrate the validity of these points and should provide illumination for future reform efforts.

The 1985 special convention (often referred to by the media and within the membership as the "integrity convention") was a striking success and demonstrated the importance of the leadership of the presidents commission. While the legislation adopted (dealing primarily with strengthening the NCAA enforcement program and defining more explicitly the authority and respon-sibility of the CEO in institutional control of athletic programs) was not perfect, as legislation can never be, and although it has been revised since adoption, there was near-universal agreement on the basic issues in that legislation. The results of the 1987 special convention were quite different, for reasons that, in retrospect, seem obvious.

The premises on which the legislation proposed by the presidents commission for the 1987 special convention were based were not without logic or support by both the academic and athletic communities, but the issues were far more complex than those addressed at the 1985 special convention. In the short time available for preparation of the legislation, it was not possible to consider adequately the impact of the proposed changes put forward under the imprimatur of the presidents commission. Consequently, by the time of the convention there was an absence of consensus, even among CEOs, for many of the principal elements proposed. Furthermore, efforts to improve the legislation by amendments, which could perhaps be characterized as frenetic, resulted in great confusion after the convention because of the inconsistencies between legislation adopted at the convention and that which it was intended to modify.

It is not surprising, therefore, that there was a perception, promoted in part by the propensity of the media for negative reporting, that the efforts of the presidents commission to maintain the momentum for athletic reform had been thwarted. College and university presidents were subject to widespread criticism, such as that voiced by Giamatti:

> In the summer of 1987, a president's commission of the NCAA was politically pummeled in public by the athletic directors, faculty athletic representatives, and conference czars who supposedly work for the presidents. Such a spectacle did not show academic leaders possessed of guts or will or much intelligence.[39]

Such criticism, which is frequently voiced, even in scholarly publica-tions,[40] is unjustified. The problem in this instance was not usurpation of presidential authority by athletic interests. Rather, it was in precipitous action in promoting legislation that had not been carefully enough developed to identify its many flaws. An important lesson to be learned from this experience is that in devising and implementing strategies for control of abuses in intercollegiate athletics, time should be our ally and not our enemy. This is an illness that has been endemic for a century. The issues are very complex; there are no quick fixes. With regard to the criticism that "the jocks" control the NCAA by determining the vote on legislation, an additional point should be made. Each institution has one vote on all legislation affecting the association, or a division/subdivision. The president or his or her formally designated representative casts that institutional vote. Therefore, if an institution's vote is different from that desired by the CEO, the fault lies with the CEO, not with the NCAA as the "mythical organization in Kansas City."

The presidents commission can provide more effective leadership by evaluating the experience of its first five years and changing certain ways in which it functions. It is obvious from the experience of the special convention of 1987 and the regular convention of 1990 that more time needs to be spent on the development of changes in legislation before they are proposed to the membership and promoted by the commission. The expanded legislative calendar now in place will provide the mechanism for accomplishing this, but cannot assure that it will be done. Of even greater importance is the need for the presidents commission to use more fully the resources of the NCAA council and various standing and special committees to evaluate alternatives for achieving objectives for which the commission has secured support at the institutional, conference, and national levels. This emphasizes the importance of CEO leadership in achieving consensus on institutional positions consistent with the goals and objectives being promoted nationally. The importance of consensus development for changes essential for reform is evident from recent reports of statements by coaches and an athletic director (of Division I-A institutions), to which reference has already been made.[41]

Because they are ultimately responsible for control of athletics on their individual campuses, CEOs must join together in determining the national goals, and the presidents commission must provide the leadership in articulating and promoting those goals. Having established the goals, the commission should then secure the assistance of those individuals and groups most knowledgeable about the complexities of the problems and the ramifications of proposed actions in developing the strategic plan to effectively control this illness that has persisted for a century.

It is now time for the presidents commission to have an independent staff executive to interface with the NCAA staff, from whom most data and history will continue to be secured, to maintain more effective communication with commission members, other CEOs, national educational organizations, and other entities. The addition of such a staff executive should not portend a functional independence of the presidents commission from the NCAA. Rather, it should be viewed as a way to enhance the effectiveness of the function of the commission within the NCAA.

*The presidents commission was established because there was a percep-
tion that presidents did not have the means to play a definitive role in
intercollegiate athletics. What we were doing was saying, "We are going
to have forty-four presidents who are going to give some time and
attention to this matter, act as kind of overseers for the rest of us, and keep
us informed about what the issues are, about what actions we ought to
be taking, and what we ought to support."*

Not only is it necessary to have better legislation, designed to eliminate
or lessen the effect of specific causes of abuses; that legislation must be more
effectively and efficiently communicated to and, when necessary, interpreted
for the membership in order that those responsible for compliance can be kept
informed about the multitude of regulations governing their activities.
Significant progress has been made in this area in recent years. Examples
include the revision of the *NCAA Manual*, computerization of interpretations,
improvements in the interpretation process, and establishment and utilization
of the conference-liaison program. The legislative review committee established
in 1989 will provide a resource for promoting these and related changes,
including further rules simplification and deregulation as the partnership
between institution, conference, and NCAA is strengthened.

In the same vein, reference should also be made to the progress
achieved in providing needed flexibility in such areas as waivers of the
freshman eligibility requirement and extra benefit regulation when circumstances warrant and when such actions will not erode the integrity of NCAA
regulations. Actions of this type—which result in fairness for individuals
without disadvantage for those against whom the affected individuals
compete—should, in the long run, gain greater respect for NCAA legislation
and more diligent adherence to it.

In spite of the best efforts of individuals and institutions to prevent
problems, there are times when corrective actions are required. It is in such
instances that the enforcement process must be brought to bear and
appropriate penalties imposed, with the objective not simply to be punitive
but to use corrective action to deter further wrongdoing. Most of those
knowledgeable about the NCAA enforcement program will agree that
progress has been made in recent years in making the process more equitable.
Of particular significance is the continuing trend toward making investigations
of an institution's program more cooperative and less adversarial.

There is one area of the investigation process, however, in which change
in the enforcement process is urgently needed. Under current policy and
procedure, the NCAA enforcement staff issues a notice of preliminary inquiry
in which the institution's CEO is advised that information has been developed
indicating that violations of the association's governing legislation may have
occurred and, therefore, that further investigation involving the use of an
enforcement representative is required. If such an investigation continues

beyond six months, the CEO is advised of this, and continuation of a preliminary inquiry beyond twelve months requires concurrence of the Committee on Infractions. If sufficient evidence is found to warrant a formal investigation, the CEO is sent a notice of official inquiry to this effect. In the notice of preliminary inquiry the CEO is told nothing about the alleged violations, only that a preliminary investigation is being initiated.

This practice, a carryover from the historically punitive nature of the enforcement program, is untenable in the present environment. In view of the potential damage to an institution from major violations and a full-scale investigation, the CEO of any institution is entitled to know immediately of any alleged violation reported to the NCAA, in order that he or she may undertake an internal investigation, with the help of the conference (if applicable) and the NCAA, in order to identify and correct any problem at the earliest possible moment. Furthermore, this immediate notification should be provided before the NCAA initiates any investigation. This is particularly true in view of the fact that an institution is obligated under current NCAA legislation to self-report to the NCAA every violation, regardless of how minor, that it detects—along with a report of the actions taken to prevent recurrence of such violations.

The rationale for continuation of this outmoded practice is that to inform an institution before definitive evidence is developed could encourage its officials to "go underground" and cover up their wrongdoing. Such logic is not defensible under present conditions, especially when greater trust is being called for in the control of abuses in college sports. Trust requires joint effort. Every CEO asked about this practice agreed that it should be changed, with appropriate consideration for the sensitivity related to the increasing prevalence of open-record laws. The following comments by several CEOs are illustrative of their views:

I want to know immediately anything that's reported about our program, and I want to know the day it is reported.

We desperately need mutual trust between the CEOs and the NCAA, and for the NCAA to say, "We don't trust you," and then demonstrate that they don't trust the CEOs by holding out on them while they go scurrying around, that's just not conducive to a strong cooperative relationship.

Until an institution or CEO demonstrates an inability or unwillingness to act, the benefit of the doubt ought to be with the institution or CEO — to look at whatever the situation is and deal with it rather than waiting for accumulation of additional evidence. Any exception not dealt with appropriately or effectively ought to be dealt with exceptionally rather than have the rule based on it.

...if for no other reason than because of the incalculable harm that takes place during the delay, while this is all in the press and everyplace else, when you don't know a thing and are like a sitting duck.

Another related action that should be taken in the area of enforcement is for the NCAA to take the initiative in developing a memorandum of understanding with each conference, at least in Division I, specifying how the conference's compliance/enforcement program interfaces with the NCAA enforcement program. This would help prevent misunderstanding and would assure greater cooperation when there is need for any investigation. For an institution to control effectively its athletic program with the greatest efficiency and expediency, it is imperative that there be a true partnership between institution, conference, and NCAA.

Finally, there is an expanded role for the NCAA to play, as there is for conferences, in helping to inform the public about the nature of the causes of abuses in college sports and about the role of the public in helping institutions control these. This can best be done by greater cooperation with the various national organizations coordinating higher education, in all its diversity, in our nation.

Conference

Some institutions, including some with big-time sports programs, have no conference affiliation and are referred to in the athletic community as "independents." Some of these, however, are aligned with conferences for selected sports (e.g., basketball) for such benefits as scheduling of contests and the opportunity for championship competition.

The conference can assist its member institutions in controlling abuses in their sports programs in a variety of ways, not all of which are directly related to compliance in a technical sense. For example, a conference plan for equitable distribution of bowl, tournament, and television revenue accruing to member institutions for their participation in featured programs under contracts negotiated by the conference can help provide financial stability and reduce somewhat the pressures to win in order to acquire such revenues. In a similar way, the assurance of some exposure in a conference television package can help balance the pressures for visibility relative to recruiting advantage.

Conferences play a major role in developing trust and promoting ethical behavior through meetings of peer groups. They are extremely important in the education of institutional personnel about NCAA legislation and its interpretation, with emphasis on common understanding and application of the plethora of complex regulations. Conferences also play a major role in helping member institutions inform student-athletes about prevailing regulations; about the dangers of gambling, unethical professional agents, and drug abuse; and about the importance of adherence to basic ethical values in their behavior.

Conferences also have a very important role to play in compliance and enforcement activities. A number of the activities identified above are indeed designed to help achieve compliance by prevention. It is not necessary for all conferences to have the same type of enforcement program, but all major conferences should have formal enforcement programs that include assistance for member institutions in their internal investigations when there is any reason to suspect impropriety in the conduct of the athletic program. In this role, the conference serves as the interface with the NCAA to achieve the three-way partnership that is essential for compliance to be effective.

Conferences, especially those whose members conduct major football and basketball programs, have generally been willing to live with minimal national standards adopted by the NCAA membership in order to avoid any competitive disadvantage. On some issues this is understandable, but the time is ripe for conferences to act more responsibly and thus serve as catalyst for accelerating the momentum for reform.

Well, I think one of the real positive things about conferences would be for the presidents to play a more active role in those conferences, to set common standards so that a conference can say, "You know, these standards that we set for ourselves go beyond the NCAA standards. These are the standards that we want to hold ourselves to in terms of what we teach at our institutions and we feel that this will help us define the appropriate competition in our conference." I think that can be a real strong emphasis for helping keep a reasonable set of limits for intercollegiate athletics when presidents come together and say, "OK, I'm going to hold my institution to these standards," and they know that others are agreeing and are doing that.

I think that the only way we're going to achieve reform is for the larger and respected conferences to decide that this is a serious enough problem that they're going to take steps within their own conferences and start controlling that. The NCAA will not be able to get all its membership to do it at one time; it just won't happen. But it would be possible for the Big-10, the Pac-10, and the SEC and the ACC, for example, to come together and say, "Look, let's start putting some things in place; yes it may penalize us when we go out and play an independent or play somebody from some other conference. We aren't going to be able to change scheduling, but at least we'll be able to look ourselves in the mirrors and know we're doing some things that are right." I think when we start doing that and putting academic progress requirements in place and maybe examine such things as freshman eligibility and begin to think about what signals we're sending out to the world when we pay some of these salaries to head coaches and so forth, yes it's going to mean a few years of diminished capabilities on the field, but I think in the long run it's the only way we're going to accomplish some of these objectives, even though in the short term there may be some disadvantages.

Finally, the conference can be extremely important in helping the general public understand the proper relationship of college sports and higher education, with emphasis on the priority of education in the mission of the university and on the importance of ethical behavior of all who are a part of higher education in our nation. To date, conferences have paid little attention to this mission, and this is understandable, given the many other demands on the resources available to them. However, they must give this a greater priority in the future as they work to help secure consensus, both regionally and nationally, on the critical issues facing intercollegiate athletics.

One of the most encouraging signs of commitment to reform, and of a willingness to implement major changes necessary to make it a reality, is the cooperative effort now under way by all major Division I conferences to identify and reach consensus on those issues on which the need for change is most urgent. This cooperative effort has been initiated by conference commissioners who recognize the necessity for reform and the contributions that major conferences can make in bringing this to pass. The commissioners of these conferences, who are being assisted by athletic directors and faculty athletic representatives, are working with the NCAA presidents commission and council in developing proposals for appropriate changes in legislation on which consensus is reached. This activity is evidence that the blanket criticism of athletic directors, conference "czars," and faculty athletic representatives is not justified.

THE ROLE OF NATIONAL EDUCATIONAL ORGANIZATIONS

Because "To reform intercollegiate athletics is to begin to approach, again, a true examination of American higher education's nature and purpose,"[42] national educational organizations must play a role in that reform. That fact is even more obvious when it is apparent, as it now is, that the abuses in college sports are not limited to the 250 to 300 institutions as perceived by Giamatti. The most widely publicized abuses have occurred in fewer than 300 institutions, indeed fewer than 100; but, as we have already documented, it is quite clear that many of the same abuses are occurring in institutions that definitely do not have big-time sports programs. Particularly disturbing in this respect is the fact that a number of Division III institutions are now admitting student-athletes who do not meet the requirements for freshman eligibility in Division I or II. If this trend continues, as it almost certainly will, absent the adoption of freshman eligibility requirements by Division III, the result will be the erosion of academic credibility of institutions that have long been considered to be the "bastion of purity" in college sports.

These abuses in institutions that do not have big-time sports programs, which appear to be increasing in frequency, may well provide the most striking evidence that higher education has not addressed effectively the fundamental causes of problems in college sports and that we must engage in "a true examination of American higher education's nature and purpose" if we are to achieve and maintain a healthy relationship between intercollegiate athletics and higher education.[43] The word "achieve" is used intentionally, rather than "restore," to focus on the critical question of whether higher education and college sports have ever had a truly healthy relationship in our nation. The history of the past century raises serious doubt about this. Higher education must address the collision of missions of these two cultures. Universities have become entertainment centers, in response to public demand, and the problems associated with this have been exacerbated by explosive commercialism. Higher education has not learned how to handle this. The situation is complicated by the fact that it is easier to cheat today.

I think we began to lose something in this country years ago in our teaching, in our families, and in the churches. Everything came up for grabs. . . . and the principles did not seem to be there. You can more comfortably cheat today because the values are just not there. People will cheat, not just for money, but for power, fame and glory. Regardless of whether they've got a million dollars, if you can beat the other guys and be number one, in the minds of many it makes a lot of sense to do so. I see that even in Division III.

In such an environment, sketched so vividly by the observation of this CEO, the NCAA could not have been expected to control effectively abuses by its traditional punitive enforcement program when its relationship with national educational organizations was remarkably similar to that which characterized the athletic and academic programs in most of its member institutions: two cultures separated by a fissure of variable width.

There have been efforts by educational organizations to effect reform of college sports. Perhaps the best example in recent history is the work of the Ad Hoc Committee of the American Council on Education in building presidential consensus for Proposition 48 (the freshman eligibility requirement) and in serving as a political force to get the proposal adopted at the 1983 NCAA convention. In that instance there were signs of the dichotomy between athletic and academic cultures identified above. This was much more evident at the 1984 NCAA convention in the debate over the structure for the greater role of CEOs in NCAA governance. Fortunately the current environment is characterized by a spirit of cooperation and a recognition that national organizations representing both the athletic and academic sides of the house must cooperate in addressing the complex issues requisite in the examination of American higher education to reform intercollegiate athletics.

It is imperative that all national educational organizations demonstrate creativity and leadership in identifying ways to help make not only intercollegiate athletics but the total spectrum of college sports (including club sports and intramural sports) an integral part of higher education. This will require long-term dedication, not just a flurry of short-term activity. In addition, and this will be equally difficult, these organizations must help gain the support of media nationally to inform the general public about the character college sports must acquire, and maintain, if higher education is to fulfill its mission for our nation.

THE ROLE OF THE MEDIA

I would like to see every newspaper with a page on education as well as a sports page, but USA Today *doesn't have four sections for the heck of it. They have four sections — "Life," "Sports," "Money," and the headline-news section—because that's what people care about. Otherwise, they would have one on education.*

The whole role of the media has to be called into question in terms of the editorial policy of a paper about education—the centrality of education. . . . Obviously they want to sell papers, and sports sell papers. But if the media as institutions in our society are going to make their contributions, they're going to have to look at this.

This gross imbalance in reporting about sports and education, which is a reflection of society's values and market forces, is not the only issue that needs to be addressed. The lumping of college sports together with professional sports deprives the reader of an essential context: when one reads about problems with University X's football team, his or her frame of reference is Pro Franchise Y in the next column, not the university's medical school at the other end of the paper. In a very subtle way, this increases the separation of the two cultures and makes more tenuous their relationship in our colleges and universities.

There are many ways in which the media can help inform the public about the primacy of quality education and the importance of ethical conduct in athletics. Several of these have been identified incisively by a senior sports editor for *Sports Illustrated*, who states, "In general . . . the media have failed college sport and, because of this failure, are as much to blame for the moral and ethical wasteland intercollegiate athletics have become as the people who break the rules."[44] This writer attributes much of the failure of the media to the fact they have not applied the same journalistic standards to athletics that are applied to such other major fields as politics, business, and science, due in part to the fact that many sports reporters have been co-opted by the perquisites received from athletic organizations whose activities they are reporting.

Among the recommendations for changes made by the writer are the following:

- Reconciliation of the conflict between being the conscience of intercollegiate athletics while acting as one of its principal publicity engines
- Addition of more investigative reporters in sports departments
- Cessation of promoting gambling interests (i.e., publishing betting lines for illegal gambling)
- Providing more balanced coverage to women and minorities in sports

There is perhaps no more conspicuous example of the conflict between serving as the conscience of intercollegiate athletics and using the publicity about sports to promote its own vested interest than in the voluminous reporting about recruiting of football and basketball players. It is the responsibility of the media to inform the public about the excesses of college sports. However, to do so while at the same time contributing to that excess is to be guilty of the same hypocrisy for which higher education is being criticized.

There is another way in which the media, particularly newspapers, should be more objective in their reporting: the clarification of certain NCAA regulations that are the subject of debate and that evoke strong emotional reactions. An example is the explanation of the requirements for a "partial qualifier" to which reference was made in the quotation by a CEO in the previous chapter. Another is the financial-aid provision for Division I, which currently permits a student-athlete who demonstrates need (under congressional methodology) to receive an amount up to an additional $1,400 during the academic year in addition to the full athletic scholarship, provided this does not exceed the cost of attendance as calculated for all students at that institution.[45] Therefore, contrary to the widely held perception, needy student-athletes who receive Pell grants are getting funds for "incidental expenses" in addition to the athletic scholarship (tuition, fees, room, board, and required books) equal to the old "laundry money" allowance adjusted for inflation. Furthermore, in calculating the amount of Pell grant funds for which the student-athlete qualifies on the basis of need, the amount of the athletic scholarship is not included as a part of family resources available to the student. An adequate explanation of financial-aid provisions could obviously affect the perception of the public about the need for student-athletes to have an incidental-expense allowance.

Much has already been said about the importance of consensus development, and the roles of individual CEOs, the NCAA presidents commission, athletic conferences, and educational organizations in achieving that consensus. At this point in the reform movement, the media can be the strongest force in helping these entities in that effort by creating an awareness on the part of the public of the pressing need to control abuses in college sports and of the changes that must be made to accomplish this. In view of the place college sports occupy in American culture, it is not realistic to expect enthusiastic support from some athletic constituencies for certain changes that will be necessary. However, widespread acceptance of these can be secured when the benefits to be derived from the enhanced quality of education that will result from effective control of this long-endemic illness are understood. The media can play a tremendously important role in helping achieve consensus and in eliciting support for the major changes that must be effected.

NOTES

1. Elaborations of these three proposals may be found, respectively, in Allen Guttmann, *A Whole New Ball Game* (Chapel Hill: University of North Carolina Press, 1988); Paul R. Lawrence, *Unsportsmanlike Conduct: The National Collegiate Athletic Association and the Business of College Football* (New York: Praeger, 1987), pp. 144-148; and Dick Kazmaier, "How Everyone Can Win in College Sports: A Pre-Professional Program for Athletes," *Chronicle of Higher Education* 35 (May 24, 1989), p. B2.

2. For a discussion of the tax implications for college sports programs, see John R. Thelin and Lawrence L. Wiseman, *The Old College Try: Balancing Academics and Athletics in Higher Education*, ASHE-ERIC Higher Education Report 4 (Washington, DC: ERIC Clearinghouse on Higher Education, School of Education and Human Development, The George Washington University, 1989), pp. 43-50.

3. The comparison appears in an article by William Gerberding, president of the University of Washington, "College Sports: Maybe They Should Pay for Play," *Washington Post* (September 5, 1989), p. A19.

4. An admirable condensation of this thesis may be found in Allen Guttmann, "The Belated Birth and Threatened Death of Fair Play," *Yale Review* 74 (Summer, 1985), pp. 525-537. The argument also appears in Gerberding, "College Sports," as does

the "shimmering ideal" figure quoted on p. 64 in the present text. Gerberding's denunciation of our misconceptions about amateurism and its connection with college sports loses some of its force in his own questionable comparison of universities with sports programs to professional "farm clubs," implying a relationship between higher education and, say, the NFL, in which undergraduate student-athletes are no more than commercial properties.

5. "The Fans Speak," *Parade* (July 2, 1989), p. 24. The question posed: "Major college sports bring in millions of dollars each year for their schools. Yet college athletes go unpaid and often receive inferior educations. Should athletes be paid for playing college sports?"

6. The analogy of parasitism and college sports is not perfect (as few analogies are), in that some benefits do accrue to institutions despite the harmful effects of abuses in athletics. However, this analogy does accurately reflect important concepts about abuses in college sports that medical metaphors help us understand. First, there are gradations of damage to the host, from the inapparent to the fulminating. Characteristics of both the parasite and the host can influence the severity of the illness and degree of damage. Thus it is apparent that the manifestations characteristic of parasitism must be neutralized and those of mutualism must be promoted to achieve what can be viewed as a healthy relationship between intercollegiate athletics and higher education—one in which the host (i.e., the university) is not harmed.

7. The revised *NCAA Manual* adopted in January 1989 is not only more easily read and understood; it includes for the first time explicit acknowledgment of principles of particular significance for the control of abuses in college sports. Among these are "The Principle of Student-Athlete Welfare. Intercollegiate athletics programs shall be conducted in a manner designed to protect and enhance the physical and educational welfare of student-athletes" and "The Principle Governing Playing and Practice Seasons. The time required of student-athletes for participation in intercollegiate athletics shall be regulated to minimize interference with their opportunities for acquiring a quality education in a manner consistent with that afforded the general student body." *NCAA Manual, 1989-1990* (Mission, KS: National Collegiate Athletic Association, March 1989), pp. 3, 4.

8. Findings in one recent infractions case provide several examples of deficiencies in administration and monitoring of the athletic program that allowed major violations to occur and that resulted in significant penalties for the institution. One of the most conspicuous of these was the fact that the head football coach was the only person responsible for the determination of the number of financial-aid awards in football. As reported by the NCAA infractions committee, the coach did not understand the NCAA regulations governing financial-aid awards for football squad members, and each year for three years more initial and overall awards had been made than permitted by the regulations.

A more salient example of institutional dereliction in the monitoring of the athletic program may be seen in recent cases in which abuses that could have been identified by a rigorous monitoring program continued even though the institutions had made commitments, following violations and the imposition of penalties during the previous decade, to establish more effective management and monitoring programs. In certain cases, it was revealed that these commitments were not kept or that effective control was exercised only during the probationary period and then relaxed.

9. The following constitute the principal areas of rules compliance to which attention must be given in the monitoring program: (1) all aspects of eligibility certification of individual student-athletes; (2) financial-aid award limitations for each student-athlete and in each sport; (3) recruiting records, for both off-campus contacts and on-campus entertainment; (4) sports camp records; (5) awards to student-athletes, by both institution and external constituencies; (6) athletic program receipts and expenditures; and (7) findings relative to all alleged improprieties, for which prompt internal investigation must be conducted when warranted by preliminary review.

10. Clark Kerr and Marian L. Gade, *The Guardians: Boards of Trustees of American Colleges and Universities: What They Do and How Well They Do It* (Washington, DC: Association of Governing Boards of Universities and Colleges, 1989), pp. 57-60. In their study, Kerr and Gade drew on information derived from interviews with approximately 850 people experienced in the operation of the university presidency and an additional 200 interviews concentrating more exclusively on the conduct of boards. In addition, for this study 1,400 individuals completed an extensive questionnaire. These were people who in 1987 were serving as board chairs, presidents, or heads of campus faculty organizations (p. 4).

11. Ibid., pp. 94-95.

12. L. Jay Oliva, *What Trustees Should Know About Intercollegiate Athletics*, (Washington, DC: Association of Governing Boards of Universities and Colleges, 1989). AGB Special Report.

13. "The Role of Faculty in the Governance of College Athletics: A Report of the Special Committee on Athletics," *Academe* 76 (January-February 1990), pp. 43-47.

14. The NCAA requires each member institution to designate an individual (faculty or administrator with faculty rank) as faculty athletic representative. The responsibilities of this position are determined by the institution. For a detailed description of the general responsibilities of the faculty representative for athletics, see: *The Faculty Athletics Representative: A Handbook* (Mission KS: National Collegiate Athletic Association, April 1987).

15. Doug Single, "The Role of Directors of Athletics in Restoring Integrity to Intercollegiate Sport," in *The Rules of the Game: Ethics In College Sports*, ed. Richard E. Lapchick and John B. Slaughter (New York: Macmillan, 1989), p. 153.

16. Ibid., p. 199. See also: "After the Cheers: Is Higher Education Serving Its Student-Athletes?," an interview with Richard E. Lapchick, by Ted Marchese, *American Association for Higher Education Bulletin* 42 (February 1990), pp. 3-8.

17. See Single, "The Role of Directors," p. 160. The urgency of the need for equity is evident from data presented by Lapchick in "Race on the College Campus," in *Rules of the Game* (pp. 68-69), where a survey of 277 institutions showed that only 266 of a possible 7,738 jobs from coach to trainer were held by blacks. R. Vivian Acosta and Linda Jean Carpenter report, in "Women in Intercollegiate Sport: A Longitudinal Study—Thirteen Year Update, 1977-1990" (available from the authors at Brooklyn College, Brooklyn, NY 11210), that only 47.3 percent of

coaching positions of women's teams in NCAA institutions are held by women and that no females at all are involved in the administration of 30.3 percent of women's programs.

18. Jack Bicknell, "The Coaching Responsibility," in *Rules of the Game*, p. 150.

19. Bicknell, "The Coaching Responsibility," in *Rules of the Game*, p. 138.

20. Derek Bok, *The President's Report, 1986-1987, Harvard University.*

21. Quoted in the *Birmingham News*, (January 25, 1990), p. F6.

22. See Robert Wilson, "Worried About 'Anything Goes' Moral Code, Colleges Are Stepping in to Help Students Shape Values," *Chronicle of Higher Education* 36 (January 3, 1990), pp. 1, A28. This is a report on selected programs initiated by colleges to assist undergraduates generally to shape their values.

23. Allen L. Sack, "Recruiting: Are Improper Benefits Really Improper?" in *Rules of the Game*, pp. 71-82.

24. *Comments from Students in the 1987-1988 National Study of Intercollegiate Athletics* (Palo Alto, CA: Center for the Study of Athletics, American Institutes for Research, August, 1989). Report 6 of the studies commissioned by the NCAA.

25. Gary R. Roberts, "Racism, Education, and Intercollegiate Athletics," *Sports Lawyer* 7 (Fall 1989), pp. 9-10.

26. A. Bartlett Giamatti, *A Free and Ordered Space: The Real World of the University* (New York: W. W. Norton, 1988), pp. 191-192.

27. The "special admission" of student-athletes who do not meet the minimum academic requirements of the general student body is a complex educational and social issue. A strong argument can be made for special admission of students with exceptional talent in a variety of areas, including athletics. In the context of reform of college sports, however, the social responsibility of colleges and universities to do this is justified only when the student-athlete has adequate academic preparation to have a reasonable chance of success in the institution in which he or she is admitted. This "reasonable chance of success" will depend on the combination of ability and desire on the part of the student and appropriate academic support and motivation provided by the institution (in the full spectrum from coach to faculty). For these reasons, institutions must do a far better job of designing, implementing, and evaluating their academic-support services, with specific attention to the criteria to be applied for "special admits" and the institution's success rate for them.

28. Richard D. Schultz, "State of the Association Address," *NCAA News* (January 10, 1990), pp. 3, 6.

29. *Comments from Students in the 1987-1988 National Study of Intercollegiate Athletics*, p. 5.

30. Striking evidence of this is seen in the data from the NCAA-sponsored report 4, *Women in Intercollegiate Athletics at NCAA Division I Institutions* (Washington, DC: American Institutes for Research, July 1989), pp. 32-34. It was found that there was no difference in the amount of time men and women basketball players spent in their sport each week, but the women spent more time (about five hours per week) preparing for and attending class than did the men. That additional time was taken from social activities and relaxing alone.

31. See "Many Colleges Move to Restrict Alcohol-Related Ads in Student Papers, Vendor's Sponsorship of Events," *Chronicle of Higher Education 36* (February 21, 1990), pp. A39-40. As reported in this article, "Administrators argue they can't enforce strict policies prohibiting underage students from drinking while allowing college newspapers to run advertisements that promote the practice." Examples are given of institutions that have taken steps to ban alcohol-related advertisements or limit alcohol promotions on their campus.

32. *The White House Conference for a Drug Free America: Final Report* (Washington, DC: United States Government Printing Office, June 1988), pp. 22, 105-107.

33. Joe Paterno, "To Turn Pro Early or Not: They Shouldn't Be Hostages," *New York Times* (January 21, 1990), p. 27.

34. *NCAA Manual*, 1989-1990, p. 4.

35. This proliferation of rules is an increasing source of frustration, especially to coaches; but they recognize their necessity in the current environment, as seen by the following comment by Bo Schembechler: "They are a pain in the butt, these rules—and every one of them is necessary." Bo Schembechler and Mitchell Albom, *Bo* (New York: Warner Books, 1989), p. 238.

36. Jack Falla, *NCAA: The Voice of College Sports, A Diamond Anniversary History, 1906-1981* (Mission, KS: National Collegiate Athletic Association, 1981), pp. 17, 31.

37. Ibid., pp. 126, 128.

38. Ibid., pp. 132-133.

39. Giamatti, *A Free and Ordered Space*, p. 191.

40. See, for example, criticisms by Thelin and Wiseman, in *The Old College Try* : "True control of the NCAA rests with athletic directors and the single faculty representative allowed each member institution" (p. 69) and "The NCAA remains largely an athletics directors' world, shared with a few long-term, visible FARs and the NCAA staff " (p. 89). Negative reporting and superficial judgments have contributed to such perceptions, which would be challenged by those with extensive firsthand experience with the governance of NCAA during the past decade.

41. See note 10 for chapter 1.

42. Giamatti, *A Free and Ordered Space*, p. 191.

43. Just as the term "illness" may signify a range of conditions as widely separated as the common cold and fatal cancer, the term "health" may connote a comparable range from that of only the absence of overt disease to that of superior fitness and well-being. In the reform of intercollegiate athletics, the immediate goal is to be free of overt illness, but the ultimate goal for a "truly healthy relationship" is to move ever closer to a supreme state of health.

44. Sandy Padwe, "The Media's Responsibility in College Sport Coverage," in *Rules of the Game*, pp. 123-135.

45. Effective in the academic year 1990-1991, the amount will be $1,700.

Chapter 4

Prescription Refinement: Improving the Prognosis

The ultimate success or failure of the reform movement in college sports will depend on the combined efforts of the constituents identified in the preceding chapter. The analysis of the pathology of infractions shows that in spite of the alienation that characterizes the relationship between athletics and education, especially in institutions with big-time sports programs, an institution can prevent gross abuses that would be characterized as major violations of NCAA legislation. But the abuses causing so much damage to the credibility of higher education are not limited to such violations. They include, as specified in the definition given in the introduction to this book, the abdication of institutional responsibility for the welfare of student-athletes, which can manifest itself in different ways and may persist as a clinically silent form of illness. The continuing disclosure of corruption, the spread of the illness to an increasing number of programs, and the well-documented deleterious effects of current practices on student-athletes show that higher education and American society have not adequately addressed the fundamental causes of this problem. More ingredients are needed in the prescription if the prognosis for reform is to be improved.

Recognizing this, NCAA executive director Schultz, in his State of the Association Address to which reference was made in the preceding chapter, challenged the membership to develop a "new model" for intercollegiate athletics, to demonstrate to the academic community and the public that college sports can be effectively controlled. That new model, so urgently needed, cannot be created overnight, and frantic efforts to do so can be counterproductive — evoking strong resistance to change from various constituencies of college sports that are determined to maintain the priorities now assigned to "their" programs.

The prescription for the reform that this model is designed to achieve must not only be comprised of the proper substance; it must be developed through a process that will lead to support by those with conflicting interests who must cooperate in making the new model function properly. Essential features of that process have been discussed in the earlier section on the role of the NCAA, but the importance of the feature of *achieving consensus* must again be emphasized. If that approach is followed, the prognosis is favorable, despite the bleak record of the many efforts over the past century to control abuses in intercollegiate athletics. However, a favorable prognosis can be sustained only if dramatic legislative changes that focus on the fundamental causes of these abuses are adopted and implemented at least by the mid 1990s, while the motivation that has brought the higher-education community to this point is still strong. A delicate balance will be required to achieve this. The reform movement must proceed with deliberate speed, but frantic efforts from which seriously flawed legislation emanates must be avoided.

Much of the substance of the prescription for reform consists of major changes in NCAA legislation necessary to create an environment in which the institution, with the help of its allies, can be more effective in preventing abuses. Each change must be evaluated by this litmus test: does it promote the primacy of education in the mission of the university, the effective integration of athletics into education, or the enhancement of student-athlete welfare? Many elements of NCAA legislation must be changed, some radically. Consequently, much effort must be exerted initially and refinement of revisions will be required as experience is gained with the functioning of the new model. The topics discussed below illustrate the breadth and complexity of the legislative issues that must be addressed.

ACCREDITATION, CERTIFICATION, AND PEER REVIEW

I'm intrigued by the possibility of an accreditation process for the whole athletic program because the nature of some violations is really academic. I believe the NCAA needs to work closely with some regional accrediting association to try to get that muscle involved in academic and athletic integrity.

The accrediting system can give the president fortitude and strength so that a board isn't manhandling a president.

I like the whole discussion about accreditation in the athletics area; it provides a great opportunity for objective review of programs. While accreditation reviews are not so enlightening or penetrating that they address every issue on the campus, they do tend to identify where the sores are and where the major problems are; and I think the accreditation process in athletics could be very, very helpful where you've had continuing board and administration problems, or it's some specific coaching problem. Whatever it is, I think they would be able to identify those kinds of issues and just stick them out there to be addressed. Just sticking them out there to be addressed would be helpful. Very often some of those things go on and on, and no one can figure out a way to begin to address them. They know what they need to do, but no one can figure out what the catalyst is to identify it as a problem. No one even wants to talk about it as a problem; it's too painful.

Because gross abuses in athletics severely damage institutional credibility, arguments have been advanced in recent years that regional accrediting agencies should remove an institution from accredited status when its program fails to meet minimum standards of propriety. Such action would result in public examination of the relationship of athletics to the total university activity, along with activities such as research and student services. It would also provide tremendous motivation for internal scrutiny because of the potential for aspersions to be cast on those who work there and those who graduate.

I read in Time *magazine that an unnamed regent of the University of _____ was heard to say [regarding their special program for student-athletes], "this could now be serious; we might lose our accreditation." All the rest didn't seem serious, but all of a sudden the notion of the higher-education community's view of his institution started to gain some weight. I don't believe there are any Division I-A institutions that could stand it very long if it were known across the country that no chief executive officer of any stature would be willing to take the job there. Regardless of how much money they have or how strong their political control of the legislature, you can't embarrass an institution that way and survive.*

Nevertheless, the issue is complex, and implementation of such a process will require much study. First, a distinction must be made between "accreditation," as currently practiced by regional accrediting agencies and professional disciplines, "certification," as used in the voluntary program initiated in 1990 by the NCAA on an experimental basis, and "informal peer review," a process employed by a number of institutions, usually on the initiative of the CEO or athletic director, for securing objective evaluation of program content or management.

Administrators have been very reluctant to submit athletic programs to peer review, either formal or informal, because of the highly competitive nature of college sports, the concern about confidentiality, and the great sensitivity about issues that might be identified. In recent years, however, the value of an informal review has been recognized by an increasing number of administrators, especially at times of change in leadership or following the identification of a major problem. In such instances, individuals with knowledge, experience, and impeccable integrity are brought to the campus to review either the entire program or specific elements of it and to make recommendations for improvements. A service of this type has been provided in recent years by the NCAA compliance-services staff, but it is not possible for the NCAA to staff at a level to continue to respond to the many requests. Moreover, individuals with more institutional experience may be of greater service to an institution. Until, and even after, more formal certification or accreditation programs are employed, and possibly mandated, informal peer review should be employed more frequently by institutions with such a need.

The voluntary certification program currently being used experimentally by the NCAA in Division I is designed to provide for an institution an objective self-examination of its athletic program, with emphasis on governance, academic standards, commitment to rules compliance, and performance and conduct of coaches and athletes. In the experimental stage, this program does not provide for punitive or disciplinary actions. It will provide guidance for the development of legislation that could mandate formal certification or accreditation programs.

If it is concluded, from further study and the experience gained from the experimental certification program, that a formal accreditation program is needed, the current model of accreditation of professional programs within universities (e.g., engineering and medicine) should be followed, with the imposition of the penalty on the deficient program, at least initially, rather than on the entire institution. Under such circumstances, conferences might prohibit member institutions from competing against an institution that had lost accreditation, and the NCAA could prohibit any athletic team or individual representing such an institution from competing in NCAA championships or certified bowl games.

While this entire matter is receiving further study, the NCAA should explore carefully the possible interface between the association and regional accrediting agencies in the implementation of formal accreditation programs. Also during this period these accrediting agencies should require institutions to provide, as a part of the ten-year accreditation renewal review, information showing an adequate comparison of the academic status of student-athletes and the student body generally. This should include detailed comparative data on admission, academic progress, and graduation rates of student-athletes, by sports.[1] Any significant deviation of the records of student-athletes from those of students generally would serve as a basis for alerting the CEO and the governing board of a real or potential problem that could erode the credibility of the institution. In addition, the institution should be required to provide the accreditation review committee a copy of the latest institutional self-study on the athletic program done in keeping with NCAA regulations and a copy of the institution's position document on its athletic program, to which reference was made in chapter 3. Any matters identified in the review of these documents that raise serious questions about the academic credibility or integrity of the institution should be addressed with the CEO in the exit session and in the written report.

In the consideration of accreditation for athletic programs, it must be remembered that, as in the academic side of the house, athletic accreditation will only help institutions identify and fulfill their own missions. It cannot substitute for that function in institutions that are unwilling to assume their own responsibility.

RECRUITING

The analysis of the anatomy of abuses has demonstrated that it is in the recruiting of prospective student athletes that the structure of intercollegiate athletics is most vulnerable to abuse. Furthermore, it is in this critical activity that the distinction between fundamental and contributing causes is most vivid.

During the past decade several refinements in the NCAA regulations governing recruiting have been made, and it is appropriate to note that a number of these have originated with coaches, motivated in large part by the desire for competitive equity and for a process that is more efficient and more easily monitored. These changes have helped improve the recruiting process, but they can be characterized as only tinkering, and more radical changes are essential if the fundamental causes of abuse are to be addressed. The recruiting process involves a balancing of the interests of prospective student-athletes, the educational institutions in which they are enrolled, and the NCAA member institutions. For this reason, the principle governing recruiting specifies that recruiting regulations shall be designed to shield prospective student-athletes from "undue pressures that may interfere with scholastic or athletic interests of the prospects or their educational institutions."[2] Thus, any changes in recruiting regulations should adhere strictly to this principle.

For this objective to be achieved, all off-campus evaluation and recruiting of prospective student-athletes by coaches and other athletic department personnel should be eliminated. Such a radical change would, of necessity, require modification of a number of other regulations involving the evaluation and recruitment of prospects and the need to provide them with appropriate information about institutions having an interest in their enrollment. However, these points are secondary to the basic rationale for such a drastic change. When blue-chip prospects (especially in football and basketball) are repeatedly called out of classes in high school to come to the coach's office to talk with college coaches who are recruiting those prospects, there can be no doubt about the greater priority being placed—by both college and high school—on athletics as the students are completing their high-school education and are considering alternative colleges in which to enroll.

Elimination of off-campus evaluation and recruiting should have two major benefits with respect to effects on prospective student-athletes: reduction of the pressures associated with intensive recruiting and promotion of a more appropriate balance between academic and athletic considerations in the student's life while still in high school and in the individual's selection of a college. There should also be less stimulation for the expansion of the egos of immature students who are highly skilled athletes and a lessening of their unrealistic expectations about their potential for athletic glory in college and beyond. The data presented in chapter 3 (p. 84) show that students' priorities in high school and in their choice of collegiate institutions, if they are to be realistic about the future, should be based primarily on educational considerations and not on their own athletic prowess.

There are other benefits to be derived from the proposed change: enhanced welfare of enrolled student-athletes and coaches and significant cost reduction for institutions. Coaches should be present on campus to fulfill their primary responsibilities as coach and teacher for their student-athletes, giving proper attention to their educational endeavors as well as to their personal and athletic development. Coaches could thus be more effective teachers, helping in a variety of ways to enhance the education of student-athletes by the integration of their athletic and academic activities. One such activity could be service on university committees addressing the matter of integration of athletics and academics. If these things are done and coaches become more effective participants in the education of their student-athletes, many of the complaints or negative reactions expressed by student-athletes in the recent NCAA-sponsored *Study of Intercollegiate Athletics*, to which several references have been made, could be redressed. Another important benefit would be the elimination of the hardship that travel imposes on the personal lives of coaches.[3] For institutions, especially in Division I-A, the proposed change would result in significant reduction in the cost of recruiting, making more of an institution's resources available for support of the sports activities themselves.

Such a radical change will evoke many objections, most of them pragmatic: (1) the coach must see prospects in competition to make an accurate assessment of their abilities; (2) it is important to visit the prospects and their parents in the home; (3) without visits in the prospects' schools and homes it is not possible to provide information the students need to make an informed decision about the schools recruiting them; and (4) such a process would provide unfair advantage for the institutions with outstanding national and regional reputations, to the great disadvantage of a young, hardworking coach of a school whose program is on the way up but has not arrived. There is an element of truth in each of these arguments, but not enough in all of them to offset the advantages to be gained by making such a change.

Coaches acknowledge that most evaluation is now being done, or can be done, by use of videotapes or movies. If deemed desirable, tests with prescribed criteria could be developed for a limited number of selected appropriate skills (e.g., speed, strength, agility, and vertical jumping from standing position), these to be administered under strictly controlled conditions to prospects on official visits to institutions and under the joint supervision of appropriate faculty specialists (e.g., exercise physiologists). For such skill tests, institutions would have no difficulty in securing appropriate insurance coverage for prospects engaged in them, and they would not involve undue stress or high injury risk of concern to high-school coaches.

Regulations could easily be changed to establish appropriate parameters for the loan to prospects of videotape cassettes with information about both the academic and athletic programs of the institution. Prepaid mailers could be included with the cassettes, and prospects could be required to return them before being eligible for an official paid visit to an institution and to return videotapes to all institutions before a national letter of intent or financial-aid agreement with any institution could be signed. Such activities could be monitored by conferences, some of which now use videotapes effectively to inform high-school student-athletes about member institutions and about conference and NCAA regulations.

There would undoubtedly be strong objection to such a recruiting process from some, but certainly not all, members of the coaching fraternity, who would perhaps be joined with vocal complaints from other interests already described. To neutralize these objections and compensate for undesirable features of such a recruiting process, there could be a change in the number of official paid visits, with the possibility of a second visit to not more than two institutions if this is needed to help a prospect resolve questions before making a formal commitment. Consideration could even be given to providing expenses for the prospect's parents on one official visit to not more than two institutions. Appropriate limitations on telephone recruiting and development of criteria for use of information from scouting services would be required. These are but examples of adjustments that could be made in NCAA regulations to overcome disadvantages of such drastic change in recruiting practices. With regard to the concern about the advantage of institutions with high program visibility, it is doubtful that those institutions would have greater advantage under the proposed changes than under current practices. It must be remembered that there can never be a perfectly level playing field.

The current state of recruiting practice is so deplorable that major changes addressing the fundamental causes of abuses in sports must be implemented. For these to achieve their objective, they should be developed by an intensive study of the several interrelated areas under a mandate by the NCAA presidents commission in cooperation with the council. Coaches, athletic directors, admissions officers, faculty, and student-athletes should participate in that study, and appropriate input should be secured from secondary-school officials. Perhaps no single change would do more to emphasize in this time of stress and anxiety about athletics and academe that a new and better relationship can be established. This would have a salutary impact not only on higher education, but also on precollege education as well.

FRESHMAN ELIGIBILITY

Whether freshmen should be permitted to compete in intercollegiate athletics has for years been a subject on which there has been wide divergence of views, and the fervor of those opposing freshman eligibility has been intensified by the recent publicity of poor academic performance and low graduation rates, especially in football and men's basketball. The complex issue of freshman eligibility has a direct link with recruiting that is far more important than generally recognized. It is frequently reported that the prospect of competing as a freshman is a major consideration in the decision of a highly recruited prospect on the institution in which to enroll. When this occurs, it is another example of athletics having higher priority than education in the choice of college for enrollment. That can have unfortunate consequences for students who fail to find the educational program they had anticipated, especially if there is the added frustration of not having the opportunity to compete as a freshman, which they had been led to expect.

Viewed only from the philosophic perspective, the issue appears quite simple: student-athletes, especially in those sports in which pressures are greatest, need to devote the freshman year to their academic pursuits and to make the necessary transition to the full spectrum of collegiate experiences if they are to balance successfully their education and athletic activities. This logic is convincing, but there are pragmatic considerations that make the question more complex than it first appears. It is this complexity that accounts for the fact that no consensus has been reached, even within the Division I membership of the NCAA presidents commission, to propose elimination of freshman eligibility.

Failure to focus the issue by defining the parameters of freshman eligibility has been one of the reasons for little progress in this debate. Can freshmen practice? If so, within what limits—in both time and type? Can they compete in freshmen or junior varsity contests? If so, how many? What limits are to be placed on strength and conditioning program activities during the first year? How many years of eligibility would the student-athlete have after the first year? Until parameters on these and related points are established, the debate can hardly be expected to be productive in leading to consensus.

Contributing to this issue's complexity is the fact that most of the research data and anecdotal evidence fail to support the view that competition as a freshman has a significant negative effect on academic retention or grade-point average during the first year.[4] However, the data from studies that have been done are not definitive because they fail to evaluate all variables that could affect the academic records of the groups studied, such as interventions employed to help student-athletes with their academic work, relative difficulty of courses taken by student-athletes and nonathletes, curriculum choice, and motivation factors.

Furthermore, the results of the *Study of Intercollegiate Athletics* conducted recently for the NCAA presidents commission show clearly that meaningful collegiate experiences that contribute to the complete education required for a lifetime of learning and productive citizenship involve far more than the intellectual development measured by number of credit hours and grade-point average. It is in social development and in preparation for life beyond the collegiate years that student-athletes may be disadvantaged most by participation in sports such as football and basketball during the freshman year.

There are still other complicating factors. Is it fair to deny opportunities for athletic participation to those student-athletes who are adequately prepared to perform well in both athletics and academics during the first year in college, simply because there are many who are not? Also, is it equitable to place restrictions of this type on student-athletes in some sports and not in others?

Yet another point must be considered in this debate. It is often affirmed that elimination of freshman eligibility would make the academic requirements for freshman eligibility moot, because eligibility for competition in the second year would then depend on the academic performance during the freshman year. Technically this might be correct, depending on the precise wording of the legislation, but this is an oversimplified view of a very complex issue. The elimination of freshman eligibility and its corresponding academic requirement would mean that each institution's determination of the criteria for "special admit" student-athletes and what academic performance would be required of them during the first year, within the minimal NCAA satisfactory-progress requirement, would be the only standard for determining eligibility during the second year. In the current environment, it is doubtful that admission standards comparable to those of Proposition 48 would continue to be imposed as widely as they currently are. Evidence shows that in many institutions the NCAA satisfactory-progress requirements for eligibility can be met without meaningful progress toward a degree, especially during the first two years. For these reasons, the elimination of freshman eligibility should not be viewed as a panacea for the problem of academic requirements for freshman student-athletes. Schultz was correct when he said, in challenging the NCAA membership to develop a new model for college sports, "We must maintain freshman eligibility standards, even if freshmen are declared ineligible."[5] That statement may be an oxymoron, but the meaning intended is certainly true.

A study of the issue of freshman eligibility in men's basketball in Division I was proposed by the Special Committee on Basketball Issues at the 1990 NCAA convention.[*] This proposal was made by the committee after it had determined, by a poll of Division I member institutions, that athletic directors and conference commissioners were almost evenly divided on the question, while coaches heavily favored making freshmen ineligible.[6] Reinforced by the results of this study, the committee reaffirmed its support of freshman ineligibility (for competition but with practice permitted) in Division I men's basketball as a way of emphasizing that the basketball community is committed to educating student-athletes and providing a better opportunity for the players to adjust socially, athletically, and culturally to the college atmosphere. It was anticipated by the committee that a study of the issue by the NCAA presidents commission and council would lead to legislation for consideration at the 1991 NCAA convention. Only one day after the debate of the issue of freshman eligibility by members of the presidents commission the membership of Division I voted not to authorize the proposed study. A number of factors probably contributed to this negative vote, but it is not unreasonable to surmise that it would have been different if the proposal had provided for a study of freshman eligibility in all sports.

The issue may indeed be most critical in men's basketball, given the widely reported low graduation rates in this sport, possibly justifying initial action in that sport only. But any study of this important issue should be expanded to include all sports. This is evident from the increasing pressures on student-athletes in all sports, as seen in the fact that the time demands on student-athletes in golf are greater than in any other sport.[7]

---

[*]This was not a formal NCAA committee, but an independent committee established by conference commissioners, athletic directors, and coaches to address a number of issues involving basketball.

While the issue of freshman eligibility is complex, the argument is unassailable that the required performance of student-athletes in most sports results in the subordination of their educational endeavors, and this in the most critical year of collegiate experience. Therefore, some restrictions should be placed on freshmen participation in all sports as a way of affirming to student-athletes, the university community, and the general public that education is the governing priority to which everything else must be subordinate in the life of student-athletes. The need is to determine by intensive study what those restrictions should be in the various sports to enhance the welfare of student-athletes and to promote proper emphasis on the primacy of education in that symbiotic relationship with athletics.

Because the pressures on the student-athlete continue beyond the freshman year, this issue should not be considered in isolation, but as a critical part of the whole. Appropriate restrictions in the freshman year and beyond would send a very powerful message about the role of intercollegiate athletics in higher education and could serve as a model for resolution of other complex issues affecting the control of abuses in college sports. As emphasized earlier, decisions about the nature of these restrictions should be made only after intensive study, involving coaches, administrators, and faculty representatives, under guidelines and objectives established by the NCAA presidents commission and council in a process that can lead to national consensus supported by institutional and conference positions.

FINANCES

Well before the first classes of the fall semester, thousands of college football players are beginning their work to extend one of the most traditional, emotional and successful illusions in the American sporting landscape: the weekly sensation that nothing has changed.

Their followers have shown a willingness to overlook artificial surfaces, 9 P.M. kickoffs, situation substitutions and scandals involving academic abuse and anabolic-steroid use because it is more pleasant to believe that for three hours on those autumn Saturdays, everything is as it has always been.[8]

The stadiums are larger, as are the bands; the games are longer, because of the frequent time-outs for television advertisements. But how much have things really changed? A careful reading of the history of college sports suggests that the changes that have occurred over the past century have been more in form than substance. The basic problems remain essentially the same, and one of the more pronounced of these has been the complex matrix of issues involving finances. Concern about the impact of commercialism on the character and integrity of athletic programs has deepened in recent years, but it has been present for a century. Among the concerns addressed at the conference of New England colleges in 1898 at Brown University were: (1) the employment of professional coaches, (2) baseball players participating in summer leagues, and (3) the impact of large gate receipts.[9]

The same concerns about finances were expressed in 1929 in the report of the Carnegie Foundation for the Advancement of Teaching:

> It may appear unjust to criticize adversely the mere size of the amounts of money involved in a year's athletics at any institution, but it is unfortunate that modern college athletics cannot be more simply and modestly conducted. High gate receipts inevitably reflect commercialism and all the evils that follow in its train. The availability of such resources stimulates from year to year the desire for steadily mounting sums that athletics, and especially athletic success, will bring.[10]

In recent years such concerns have been exacerbated by the expansion of professional sports programs and by television and corporate sponsorships, now not only of bowl games and tournaments but also of the individual games of an institution. Currently, the emphasis in many athletic programs is on creative marketing and fund development (e.g., endowments for scholarships for positions on a football team) needed to meet spiraling costs and to achieve "the financial stability necessary for providing student-athletes with adequate opportunities for athletics competition as an integral part of a quality educational experience."[11] It is not clear that there is a causal relationship between the increasing dependence on such sources of funds and the failure of institutions to make the competitive opportunities provided by those funds an integral part of a quality educational experience for the student-athletes. However, that is a possibility that must be considered carefully as institutions make decisions about fund development and allocation for their sports programs.

Many countervailing forces operate in the complex area of college sports financing, and many of these must ultimately be controlled by individual institutions; but for a number of the more important ones parameters within which that control can be achieved must be established through national consensus on constraining regulations. Initial steps to accomplish this at the 1991 NCAA convention are being recommended by a special committee on cost reduction. Further efforts will be necessary, and in addressing this issue the association should consider it carefully in the context of the interrelated fundamental and secondary causes of abuses in college sports.

The fact that at least 50 percent of Division I institutions currently have a deficit in their athletics budget is properly a cause of great concern to athletic and university administrators. Even so, the amount of money in the athletic budget is of far less importance than the ways in which the money is secured, the things for which it is spent and the processes by which budget decisions are made and controls are exercised. Unless the decisions on all of these matters are made in keeping with the principles of proper integration of athletics and education and adherence to basic ethical values by all involved in athletic programs, the seed for abuses will have been sown, and the endemic illness will not only persist but may become florid at any time.

The central point to be made is that, with all its complexity, athletic financing is not for the CEO the one-of-a-kind phenomenon it is often allowed to seem. The demands on the university president to prevent skewing of a plethora of financial relationships accounts for much of the complexity of that position in contemporary higher education as described in chapter 3. There should be no essential difference between the principles at issue in a university's appraisal of a grant from industry to support an academic program of special relevance to that industry's development and those principles involved in a grant or gift from external sources to support the institution's athletic program. The hypothetical model below, suggested by Giamatti,[12] is an example of experiences common in the nation's universities.

In the scenario, a group of senior faculty and academic administrators, possibly including the president, are assembled to discuss the issues facing the university that would result from a proposed gift of two million dollars by a major pharmaceutical company to support basic research in a discipline on the cutting edge of biomedical science. Among the issues discussed are: (1) "knowledge as property versus knowledge as a free good"; (2) "potential conflicts of time and commitment" of the senior faculty; and (3) protection of the welfare of the graduate students and postdoctoral students who would participate in the work of the project—that is, how to conduct the program "without commercializing the training of the students."

Comparable standards and procedures applied to athletic-program funding would assure institutional independence, would preclude conflicts of interest of coaches, and would protect young student-athletes from com-mercialization. The failure of universities to apply comparable standards and procedures for their athletic programs as they strive to meet multiple responsibilities to their various constituencies is evidence of the loss of memory of the relationship that should exist between intercollegiate athletics and education. Universities capable of maintaining the integrity of education as a partner of business and industry in multi-million-dollar research endeavors are capable, if the will is present, to do the same in the operation of athletic programs. As Giamatti observes, the blame for abuses related to extramural funds lies not with evil external forces but with the academic leadership of the institutions, who often are willing to take the outside funds without assuring there is no vested interest involved.[13] In the administration of athletic programs, institutions would be well advised to apply this model, which provides a perfect illustration of how universities can avoid drifting into confining relationships with commercial interests.

As the reform of intercollegiate athletics achieves its objective of bringing the athletic and academic cultures into a reciprocal relationship, the issue of use of public funds for athletics will have to be addressed more precisely than it has been. The legal prohibition or policies against this in some states may well be evidence of that fissure between the two cultures that we have chosen to disregard because of the discomfort that would result from its admission. It would, of course, be incongruous to prohibit by law the use of public funds for athletics, or to require their administration under a separate corporation to prevent the mixing of athletic and education funds, when athletics constitute an integral part of education. This is not to say that public funds should be expected to support big-time athletic programs, but rather to emphasize that the true reform of college sports will require the reexamination of many facets of their financial operation.[14]

One of the more complex issues involving finances that must be addressed more effectively, and one which needs immediate attention in the reform of college sports, is that of the grant-in-aid for student-athletes—the amount of aid to be awarded and the criteria to be followed in determining the award. Awarding aid that is based at least in part on need is more consistent with the principle of integration of athletics and education than the current method of awarding athletic scholarships without regard to need, as is done in Divisions I and II.

It has been shown that student-athletes at most institutions would receive less money if financial aid were awarded on the basis of need, using congressional methodology. Consequently most institutions would realize cost savings, the amount varying from institution to institution. The cost savings realized by the application of need-based aid would, however, be offset by additional administrative and programmatic costs. Moreover, the truly needy student-athlete would be the most severely affected by the reduction in aid to student-athletes, and the opportunity for these students to receive the full cost of attendance through the grant-in-aid program now appears to have a very high priority for both academic and athletic officials throughout the NCAA membership. Consequently, the alternative of need-based aid will not now be pursued by the NCAA as a cost-saving measure.[15]

A plan under which all aid in excess of the full-tuition and fees grant is based on need should, however, be pursued vigorously as a central feature of the reform of college sports, because few changes in NCAA legislation can have a greater impact on the psychology of student-athletes and coaches, or on the perception of those in the academic community and the public generally. Such a change would do much to promote not only the perception but the reality of amateurism and to achieve a balance between education and athletics as the student's motivation for enrollment in a collegiate institution.

There are indeed practical problems in the implementation of need-based aid. These include the difficulty of getting forms properly completed by prospects early enough to permit the determination of aid for which the prospect is eligible, the difficulty of determining early enough the precise amount of aid a prospect might receive from different institutions seeking his or her enrollment, and the possibility of cheating in the determination of the amount of aid awarded, in order to gain a recruiting advantage. These problems are real, but they are not insurmountable.

It should be possible for the NCAA to develop a program with limited criteria for determining need-based aid, one that would provide equity and opportunity for award of full cost of attendance for truly needy students. Operated by a national service supported by the NCAA and implemented in cooperation with state athletic associations and conferences, such a program would have minimal potential for abuse. This is of such importance that it should be a high priority for the NCAA in the decisions about allocation of the additional revenue to be available from the Division I basketball tournaments in 1991 through 1997, an issue that is discussed below.

Among the arguments against need-based aid and for allowances beyond those currently permitted, even beyond the full cost of attendance, is the assertion by some that football and basketball players should be entitled to share in the fruits of their labor—the millions of dollars earned by institutions in these sports by their participation. But in addition to the compelling philosophic argument against awarding aid in excess of full cost of attendance, the data presented earlier (see p. 38, chap. 2) on deficits in athletic budgets, even in Division I, show clearly the pragmatic problems of such a course of action. Furthermore, ethical and legal ramifications are obvious, since women student-athletes would be negatively impacted by such an approach.

It is not surprising that an increasing number of football and basketball coaches are calling for an increase in allowance for student-athletes in these sports. Many of the most successful coaches in these sports are themselves receiving compensation from such outside sources as television and equipment manufacturers equal to more than five times their institutional salary, which itself often approaches or exceeds the salary of the CEO. In addition many coaches receive seven-figure amenities (e.g., annuities) and houses valued at a half-million dollars or more, provided generally by alumni/booster organizations.[16]

The solution here lies not in paying student-athletes to play (i.e., granting of total aid in excess of full cost of attendance). Rather, it is in prohibiting coaches from profiting personally from the use of university resources and requiring that they not engage in extramural activities that constitute conflict of interest or a neglect of their institutional responsibilities, especially their roles as "teachers" in the comprehensive education of student-athletes. These are principles consistently applied for the approval of extramural activities for university faculty and staff, and they should be applied to coaches also.

There is compelling logic in the argument that the replay of a university's football or basketball game on television is a part of the university's program and that revenue derived from it should accrue to the university rather than to the coach, and that when members of an athletic team wear a given brand of shoes any contribution from the manufacturer should come to the university for use in its program rather than to the coach. Another aspect of coaches' compensation should be examined: contractual provisions that obligate an institution to pay multiyear commitments or amounts that would be derived from "outside income" when a coach is terminated or resigns under pressure for failure to fulfill responsibilities inherent in the position, even though there is no proof of personal involvement in major NCAA violations. Faculty, even those with academic tenure, are also subject to termination when they fail to fulfill their responsibilities, but they do not receive comparable compensation. The same principle should apply to coaches, for whom competence clearly involves far more than avoidance of criminal activity or personal involvement in major rules violations.

There is another area in which corrective action should be taken. Athletic departments of some Division I-A institutions are provided as many as fifty or more complimentary automobiles from dealers who, in return, receive free tickets to contests and other amenities, as well as extensive advertising in programs. Many of these automobiles are assigned to athletic-department staff members who have little or no need for an automobile in performing their official duties, or even to coaches' spouses. When this occurs, the university's resources are being exchanged for personal gain of staff members, and ethical principles that should guide the decisions for prudent financial management are not being followed.

Another side of the coin, in fairness, must be recognized. There are a number of examples of athletic programs that have made contributions from budget surplus to an institution's academic programs—library construction, reduction of a budget deficit, or other specific activities. This is only appropriate and should be done more often in those institutions with successful programs. One CEO suggested a logical use of such onetime largess: the purchase of equipment to enhance the academic-support or learning-resources programs for the general student body to make them more nearly comparable to those provided for student-athletes. Regardless of the use, one condition identified by several CEOs interviewed should be observed. Contributions from athletic funds should not be incorporated into recurring items of the academic budget, for if that is done there is even greater pressure on the athletic program to win and thus continue to fund those items.

NCAA STRUCTURE AND DISTRIBUTION OF REVENUE

The structure of the NCAA membership and the policies for distribution of the association's revenues can influence significantly the ability of member institutions to control abuses in college sports. The driving forces for the evolution of the current federated structure, the basic features of which were adopted in 1973, have been the desire to provide more opportunities for championships participation and to create more homogenous groupings of institutions that have the ability to control their futures by adopting regulations deemed most appropriate for the promotion of athletic programs at the level to which they have committed. The constraints on these forces have been the recognition that the goal of the membership, maintaining competitive athletic programs as an integral part of education conducted in keeping with basic principles of ethical behavior, can best be achieved through mutual effort in a strong alliance of the total membership and the fear that permitting any group to abolish all limits on such elements as financial aid could greatly disadvantage other groups.

The dynamic tensions that currently contribute to the desire for further fine-tuning of federation of the NCAA provide opportunity to achieve greater efficiency and harmony in the association's governance of intercollegiate athletics. However, harmony and efficiency must not be gained at the expense of abdication of principles required to achieve the basic purpose for which the association and its member institutions exist. That abuses in college sports have persisted as an endemic illness of higher education for a century is undoubtedly due to the fact that the association's membership, regardless of its changing structure, has not been adequately concerned about the fundamental causes of abuses in devising legislation to govern the programs conducted by institutions in the various divisions. Instead, attention has been concentrated disproportionately on matters that affect competitive equity, matters that influence significantly the contributing causes of abuses.

Athletic homogeneity will continue to be a major consideration as adjustments are made in the federated structure of the NCAA, and properly so. Just as diversity of American higher education is one of its greatest strengths, diversity in competitive levels of athletic programs can contribute to the strength of the association and to the quality of athletic programs conducted by its member institutions. But this will be true only if there is unity in commitment of the entire membership to the goal of making athletics an integral part of education. To reaffirm this commitment, the membership of each division should review carefully and make appropriate revisions in its divisional philosophy statement.[17] Adoption of an idealistic philosophy statement will not be sufficient, however; each institution must then adhere to the principles contained therein, with the assistance of other institutions and under their collective purview.

The structure of the NCAA is influenced, directly and indirectly, by the distribution of the association's resources, particularly the revenue from the Division I men's basketball tournament, which currently provides more than three-fourths of the total funds in the NCAA budget. The precipitous rise in revenue from the Division I men's basketball tournament during the past ten years (see fig. 3, chap. 2) has enticed a number of institutions to seek Division I membership. To deter such movement of institutions that more appropriately belong in Division II and to reduce the pressures to win on the basketball programs of Division I institutions generally, a number of suggestions have been made about the distribution of revenues from this tournament. The more extreme of these include expanding the tournament to include in the initial round all institutions in Division I, rather than sixty-four as in the current format, and dividing the revenue equally among all Division I institutions after only the expenses are paid for teams participating in the tournament. Neither of these is supported by compelling logic when all the philosophic and pragmatic considerations are taken into account. But changes are needed in the plan for distribution of these revenues to promote the positive features of federation and to strengthen the unifying bond that focuses on the central purpose of the alliance. An issue that has been very serious in recent years must now be characterized as critical in view of the staggering sum of $1 billion contracted for the TV-rights fees for this tournament for the seven years beginning in 1991. This is an average of approximately $143 million per year, in contrast to an average of approximately $53 million per year for each of the preceding three years.[18]

Such an impressive increase in revenue at this juncture is fortuitous in that it provides unparalleled opportunity to promote reform. For this to be accomplished, however, the NCAA membership must be willing to make changes in the way it conducts its business that are as radical as those required in the legislation governing the way their athletic programs are operated. First, a significant portion of the increased revenue should be placed in an endowment, with only the income from that used for program support. In the face of many uncertainties of the future, this will assure long-range benefits for the membership.

Second, the principle that has evolved for the distribution of NCAA championships revenue should be reexamined. This principle provides that 60 percent of the net revenue from a championship is divided among participating institutions and the remaining 40 percent goes to the NCAA for administrative costs and general program support. (The Division I men's basketball tournament is the only championship that produces significant net revenue after championship expenses are paid, and the majority of the seventy-seven national championships currently conducted produce no net revenue.) The association should consider no distribution of net revenue to participating institutions and devise appropriate criteria for allocation of resources—criteria that reward institutions for program merit rather than simply "paying for winning." Criteria that have been suggested include: number of sports sponsored, number of scholarships awarded, number of participants in championships, and graduation rate of student-athletes. Others that promote integration of athletics and education, student-athlete welfare, athletic homogeneity, and compliance with NCAA legislation can be devised, but will require very careful study and deliberation by the membership. While this is being done, much of the increase in tournament revenue can be placed in endowment as recommended above.

Third, even if the membership does not choose to eliminate distribution of all championships revenue to participating institutions, the 60:40 distribution ratio for the Division I men's basketball tournament should be discontinued. When the revenue for this tournament increased significantly for the period 1988-1990, the principle for allocating these resources was nominally maintained but was in fact circumvented by deducting from the net receipts to be distributed to participating institutions the costs for several new programs.[19] Reasons for this budget approach included uncertainty about the revenue to be derived from the tournament after 1990 and conviction that the amount distributed to participating institutions should not be higher than provided by this provisional approach. Given the amount of revenue committed for the period 1991-1997, a more forthright budgeting approach is in order. The fact that this tournament has become the nation's premier college sports event and the amount of money now generated by it are convincing arguments for treating the revenue derived from it differently from that of any other championship. This has become a truly unique NCAA property and should be treated accordingly.

When the television-rights fees for this tournament increased significantly under the contract for the years 1988-90, funds accruing to the association from that increase were used to initiate several new programs for the benefit of all institutions in Division I and indirectly those in Divisions II and III. These included:

- Conference grant programs for Division I conferences to assist in the initiation or enhancement of compliance and enforcement programs, programs for improvement of men's and women's basketball officiating, drug-education programs, and opportunities for ethnic minorities and women
- Payment of premiums for the NCAA lifetime catastrophic athletic injury insurance for all Division I men's and women's basketball players
- Allocation of eleven million dollars as seed money to launch the NCAA Foundation, the initial goals of which are to: promote enhancement of academic performance by providing scholarships to assist student-athletes who have exhausted eligibility to complete degree requirements; stimulate increased attention to the prevention, treatment, and rehabilitation of injuries from athletic participation; promote programs to prevent substance abuse; and provide graduate

fellowships for needy former student-athletes, both male and female, and particularly ethnic minorities, to better prepare them for careers in sports administration

In addition to these specific program activities supported by the increased income from the Division I men's basketball tournament, the funds available to the association during this period have made possible increased funding for the block grants for Divisions II and III that cover transportation expenses for championships in those divisions. These actions, the results of which have been very positive, provide guidance for decisions on ways the increased funding projected from the Division I men's basketball tournament for the years beyond 1990 can be used to make federation more effective while placing proper emphasis on the unifying principles of the alliance.

Even if participating teams continue to share in the net tournament revenue, there can be little disagreement that the current payoff to participating teams is adequate and should not be increased. Therefore, any increase in tournament revenue, and probably even some of that currently allocated to participating institutions (especially those in the advanced rounds), should be allocated to programs in a way that will not only promote the best interests of all Division I member institutions but also provide greater equity for institutions in Divisions II and III.

Among those areas to which high priority should be given are:

- Strengthening of Division II, especially in the sport of basketball
- Guaranteeing both transportation and per diem expenses for participants in Division II and III championships
- Extending the best possible coverage for lifetime catastrophic athletic injury insurance to all student-athletes in all three divisions
- Continuation and expansion of activities such as those in the conference programs initiated during the past three years
- Development of programs to help institutions and conferences integrate more effectively athletics and education and to emphasize adherence to principles of ethical conduct in athletic programs
- Evaluation, improvement, and expansion of programs for certification and accreditation of athletic programs, possibly in cooperation with regional accrediting agencies
- Development and implementation of a need-based aid program for student-athletes in Divisions I and II

The association should not only extend its lifetime catastrophic athletic injury insurance to cover all student-athletes in all three divisions; it should improve the coverage of that program so that it provides the best possible benefits for student-athletes within the resources available. Since the needs of institutions in the three divisions vary, in relation to the coverage provided by their institutional insurance programs, the NCAA should secure the advice of risk managers of representative institutions in each division about the provisions most appropriate for each in the NCAA program.

As recommended in the preceding section, the NCAA should explore in depth the feasibility of implementing an equitable need-based aid program for student-athletes in Divisions I and II. The responsibility for financial support of that program would logically rest with the NCAA, but the benefits to be derived would more than warrant that expenditure. By implementing such a program, in cooperation with state high school athletic associations and conferences, the NCAA would contribute to the enhancement of quality education in our nation at the precollege as well as the collegiate level.

These topics are only illustrative of the legislative issues that the NCAA must address in effecting meaningful reform of college sports. There are others. For example, many aspects of amateurism and the related question of the role of intercollegiate athletics in providing opportunities for the development of elite athletes for international competition must be reexamined. Furthermore, as changes are implemented, new problems — or old ones with new dimensions—will arise.

The number and complexity of the issues, combined with the inherent difficulty for individuals and society to accomplish major changes, make the task of reforming athletics a most difficult—and still uncertain — one. An adequate understanding of the benefits that will accrue from a wholeness in the relationship of education and athletics should serve as sufficient motivation for confronting the challenge. It is now well established in medical science that a patient's hope, confidence, and determination to achieve a favorable outcome can enhance the prospect for successful recovery from an illness — even one with a very grave prognosis. These attributes will be no less important in higher education's confrontation with this illness.

NOTES

1. Such an analysis might include more detailed data than will be a part of the public report required for all Division I and II institutions mandated by the membership at the 1990 convention. The first report using rolling five-year averages will be due for Division I institutions in October 1991 and for Division II institutions in October 1994.

2. *NCAA Manual, 1989-1990* (Mission, KS: National Collegiate Athletic Association, March 1989), p. 4. This stipulation is from the principle governing recruiting in the NCAA constitution.

3. On this point, it is pertinent to note that at the end of the 1989 season one head football coach in Division I-A and one in Division I-AA both gave as the reason for resigning their positions their unwillingness to continue to endure the rigors of recruiting. Furthermore, Bo Schembechler, who resigned as head football coach at the University of Michigan after the 1989 season, is reported to have said, "I'd probably still be in coaching if I didn't have to hit the road five days a week for ten weeks, then go home to entertain prospects on weekends." *Birmingham News* (March 25, 1990), p. C1.

4. *Athletics and Academics in the Freshman Year: A Study of the Academic Effects of Freshman Participation in Varsity Athletics*, conducted by the American College Testing Program and Educational Testing Service for the American Association of Collegiate Registrars and Admissions Officers and the American Council on Education, with the cooperation and support of the College Board (Washington, DC: AACRAO, December 1984). This study involved paired student-athletes and nonathlete students in fifty-seven institutions (public and private) representing twenty-three conferences and all eight NCAA districts. The following is an excerpt from the Executive Summary: "None of the evidence arising from the study suggests that participation in freshman athletics, in itself, has a negative effect on academic performance in the freshman year. Therefore this study provides no support for a blanket prohibition of freshman participation in college varsity athletics."

5. Richard D. Schultz, "State of the Association Address," *NCAA News* (January 10, 1990), pp. 3, 6.

6. "Basketball Group to Ask Convention to OK Freshman-eligibility Study," *NCAA News* (October 16, 1989), pp. 1, 3.

7. See William C. Rhoden, "Pro Tours Never Far in Tennis and Golf," *New York Times* (January 9, 1990), p. 48.

8. Malcom Moran, "Colleges Fight to Pay for a U.S. Tradition," *New York Times* (August 13, 1989), pp. 29, 34.

9. Ronald A. Smith, *Sports and Freedom: The Rise of Big-Time College Athletics* (New York: Oxford University Press, 1988), p. 139.

10. Howard J. Savage, et al., *American College Athletics* (New York: The Carnegie Foundation for the Advancement of Teaching, 1929), p. 88.

11. *NCAA Manual, 1989-1990*, p. 5. This is the basis for the principle governing the economy of athletics program operation in the NCAA constitution.

12. A. Bartlett Giamatti, *A Free and Ordered Space: The Real World of the University* (New York: W. W. Norton, 1988), pp. 181-183. On this point see also the earlier reference (note 17 of chapter 2) to Weisbrod's thesis about the general commercialization of universities.

13. Ibid., p. 185.

14. For a discussion of the use of public monies for the support of intercollegiate athletics as a public policy issue, see John R. Thelin and Lawrence L. Wiseman, *The Old College Try: Balancing Academics and Athletics in Higher Education* (Washington, DC: ERIC Clearinghouse on Higher Education, School of Education and Human Development, The George Washington University, 1989), pp. 51-54.

15. Marvin C. Carmichael, "Statement to Convention on Need-based Financial Aid," NCAA News (January 24, 1990), p. 6.

16. See Tom Junod, "Paydirt: How College Football Coaches Really Make Their Money," *Southpoint* 1(1) (October 1989), pp. 35-44, 90-94; and Keith Dunnavant, "Perks Put College Coaches in Clover," 208(18) *Sporting News* (October 23, 1989), p. 56.

17. NCAA Manual, 1989-1990, pp. 282, 288, and 291-292.

18. The discussion below on the distribution of revenue for the Division I Men's Basketball Tournament was prepared before the decision by the NCAA Executive Committee in August 1990 on the distribution of the funds (approximately $115 million) for the first installment of the CBS contract. Since decisions on allocation of funds for future years will be made annually as part of the NCAA budget process, the recommendations below, some of which are congruent with the Executive Committee's decision on use of funds of 1990-1991, are still relevant for consideration by the NCAA membership at this critical juncture. Funds from the television-rights fee will increase annually through the remaining six years of the contract, thus making absolutely necessary the development of an equitable long-range policy.

19. See Executive Regulation 31.4.7.2-(c) in the *NCAA Manual, 1989-1990*, p. 345.

Chapter 5

In the Waiting Room: The Prospect for Wholeness

The writing of prescriptions, of course, even those based on an accurate diagnosis, does not guarantee that the end of a particular case will be one of recovery. When the "patient" is intercollegiate athletics, and the "prescription," behavioral and procedural rather than medicinal, is calculated to integrate or at least bring closer together those dislocations of purpose and direction that have occurred over a century, the outcome is problematic. Prescriptions must be administered to be effective, and they cannot, of themselves, overcome resistances. The patient must not only want to get well but must have the support of friends and relatives. Obviously, in the present case, some of those closest to the patient are either hostile to any form of treatment, regarding such as intrusive or ill-informed, or else insist that the recorded incidence of disease does not constitute a serious problem. A principal purpose of this book is to obviate such judgments and, rather, to assist in elevating a joint academic-public sensibility that, first, the latent infection of college sports is widespread, and that, second, the condition can be brought within a reasonable measure of control.

The greatest deterrent, however, here at the beginning of the 1990s, to translating that elevated sensibility into corrective action may be our lack of confidence in the very concept of reform, a question embracing far more issues than that of intercollegiate athletics. A thesis of "reform" on a given issue posits a belief that a future can be created within which the conditions containing or affecting that issue will be improved. Writing recently in the *New York Times*, historian Christopher Lasch suggested that there seems little reason to conclude that in the 1990s Americans will abandon the behavioral patterns of selfishness, yuppie-greed, self-enrichment, and instant gratification characteristic of the 1970s and 1980s. For the majority of Americans, particularly those who have come to their maturity in the last forty years against a background of nuclear intimidation, urban and environmental catastrophes, and political corruption and deception, there is no sustaining rationale for a belief in the future. The problems of public education and widespread cultural breakdown in family structures have largely halted the telling of traditional stories from our common inheritance—the Bible, mythology, heroic legend—thus depriving many Americans of any connection with a historical or imaginative past against which to place their own experience.[1]

While the structural description of this sense of isolation and self-indulgent paralysis is depressingly familiar, it contains—shares, in fact, with those similar themes sounded by Barbara Tuchman fifteen years earlier—the particular virtue of asserting that telling the truth about a given condition is absolutely requisite to any possibility of reforming it. If *glasnost* is part of a "coping mechanism" on one crucial front, then indeed the continued assertion over forty years of certain international truths has helped it to emerge. The ability of science to ameliorate environmental conditions is vastly inhibited unless the truth of that certain death inherent in the instant gratification and greed represented by pollution is believed. College sports, however, even though the truth about their troubled condition now seems to be securely recognized and a tide of concern and anxiety to be steadily rising, nevertheless pose a particular enticement to nonaction simply because, as we all know, they deliver in such dramatic and celebratory ways the very sensation of instant gratification. And this sensation is often communicated by television, which encourages a short attention span and is itself the foremost enemy of the telling and reading of stories.

Once more, then, our ambivalence: our enjoyment on the one hand of the powerful superficiality of college sports, which may in itself inhibit reforms, and on the other our lament of their infected condition and thus their alienated relationship to academe. It is possible, however, that our strongest motivation toward the reform of intercollegiate athletics may be appearing fully just now, as this last decade of the twentieth century begins. Almost from their beginning, as we have seen, these games have constituted one of the widest and most immediate fellowships in our country's imaginative life. Indeed, they have assumed an irrevocable permanence at the same time that many of our traditional links with the past have disappeared, a condition of loss that higher education is now desperately and properly seeking to repair through curricular reform. This is not to say, of course, that they have displaced what have been our shared, inherited stories or that they are necessarily one of our few remaining common cultural denominators. But their extraordinary presence and our need to believe in their integrity seem now significant, perhaps crucially so in ways not possible forty years ago.

In their own way, our intercollegiate games are stories too. They are constantly being remembered and retold, some more than others, of course, but each contest seems linked in some way with the previous one and with others of the immediate past. And portions of those earlier contests are such good stories that they may be reenacted for a television viewing audience, heightening the viewers' sense of expectation as to what the new story about to begin will tell. Even now as this is being written, another year's Final Four tournament has ended, and millions of Americans have witnessed dramatic episodes from earlier tournaments and from this one—stories of sacrifice, success, and error; poignant moments of grief; ironic outcomes as those who are expected to win do not.

A mythic glance back into the dim enclosures of our ancient memory would suggest that at one time games or contests must have told one of the basic stories, perhaps the longest one that we know. Then there was no suspense among the tribal audience as to how the game would turn out. The Winter King would always lose the contest for the Spring Maiden to the warmth and rich promise of the Autumn Harvest, although his power to wound and kill would return. Today, a game's "season" usually extends beyond what were once its natural chronological boundaries, but even so the seasons of sport now rival the Christian calendar in the way we mark the stages in our annual life. And perhaps we should not be too quick to patronize the technology that in countless stadiums late on a Saturday afternoon ironically captures a vague sense of that distant reenactment of the triumph of spring over winter, as an artificial sun shines beneath the dark November sky on a playing field that is always green.

We cannot, of course, find in those games—with their emphasis on the final score—that same intrinsic story that the ceremonial competition between the circling seasons could yield: something reassuringly predictable, though still mysterious. Obviously, there is nothing mysterious about the linear computerized forms of experience that now strongly influence our behavior. The story of our statistical past can be recalled in a moment and then be sustained through a calculated model into a future that is predictable, though hardly reassuring. Our lives are now inextricably contained within the hard edges of this different kind of story, which, though indescribably useful, is yet sufficiently sterile to encourage that sense of cultural immobility characterized by searches for sensation and instant gratification. Our intercollegiate games, in their own distinctive way, oppose this story by telling contrasting ones of their own, even at the same time they are powerfully communicating a feeling of transient spectacle. For while more often than not the favorite team will win the contest, there is always the chance that it will not, or at least will be uncomfortably tested. And it is not uncommon for us to see in these games stretches of experience definitely marked by the unpredictable, where the odds are beaten, and which we can structurally describe in phrases such as "turning points," when this or that error or transcendent exploit occurred. In fact, even were we only casual observers of the NCAA basketball tournament just completed, we would have noted the relatively high number of games where winner and loser were separated by only one, two, or three points, where literally in the last few seconds a game was won or lost, tempting us to echo the judgments of the two television commentators whose dialogue in 1989 initiated the story of this book: "Incredible!" "Can you believe it?"

Bringing the message of stories such as these more closely into harmony with those traditional tales still surviving, we trust, in the other side of the university house may indeed not be the most crucial of our current cultural tasks. But college sports seem as permanent a fixture in the university environment as any academic department. And it is critical that if we are to receive fully the value of the messages they are capable of sending, then they themselves must be free of skepticism; their revelation that the odds can truly be overcome must be free of suspicion that lying behind the message is a pattern of corrupted motives and a crass and selfish manipulation of young athletes. Games must somehow thus be connected to a system of educational reciprocity, giving back to their environment a value fully acceptable, something of worth. That something of worth is not to be found in their singular capacity to entertain, in their commercial trappings, in their provision of a ceremonial setting for the school's development program, or even in their undeniable power to release in the memory of thousands of alumni a nostalgic vision of past experiences that appear increasingly less complicated and more meaningful than the hovering present.

The sense of worth must, of course, essentially be present in the personal experience of the team members, in what the game (which they unquestionably love and respect) has taught them: a sense of self-discipline, perhaps; the ability to subordinate, but not lose, the self to a group effort; a feeling of pride and accomplishment that these goals have been achieved; and, inevitably, a recognition of one of the great humanistic themes of our culture—that one may learn more from losing than from winning. But though these learning experiences occur in a public and dramatic context, they are not unrelated to the innumerable though silent transactions of personality that occur for all students each day in the college library, the laboratory, or the rooming house. And if those new understandings gained with skill, pain, and frustration on the field of play are not part of a continuum of value that extends on Monday morning into the realm of books and ideas, then all the cynical derogations of college sports are difficult to reject: that the participants, the players, are no more than hired guns performing briefly for this or that team, or a labor supply for a giant entertainment industry.

I'm not the least bit apologetic to the young warrior who goes out there and fights for alma mater on the gridiron, and it doesn't bother me if the university is bringing in a fair amount of money and he is not getting a big salary, provided *he's getting something else of tremendous value and that something else is a good education—it will last him throughout life. And if we're not giving him that, it's just exploitation.*

The anatomy of abuses in intercollegiate athletics, though conditioned and sustained by a conception of sports as commercially "useful" and by the ambivalent human motives of vanity and ambition, begin and end with our student-athletes.   Their intense and noisy recruitment and institutional passage lead on many campuses to a sequestered existence disengaged from the prevailing educational ethos, an existence often observed with benign neglect by the institution itself. Our attitude toward college sports, which are always at risk to the latent infection lying within this separated condition, may indeed reveal much about the contradictions and ambiguities that themselves are always latent in our democratic habit of mind, our longing for ideals and our inability to resist their pragmatic transformation. All of us feel cheated when our ideals of amateurism, integrity, and fair play seem betrayed as our games are held up as corrupt.

Yet it's all so ambivalent. People will say look at all those athletes, they're dumbbells and they're getting free rides and this is a disgrace—and then they'll of course put up a couple of hundred dollars for the best possible seats and never miss a game.

But as always in a democracy, there is a point beyond which our tolerance will not extend, a point, one hopes, that will never be reached: when college games cease to have relevance for our own lives. To be sure, that relevance may be obscurely embedded within the spectacular happening that a game day often becomes. Then the rapport between coach and players is at its height, and the student-athlete is center stage, filling a role toward which all the regimented hours have pointed and one that will be played out before an audience that will, to some degree, assign to the encounter an exorbitant significance and attribute of worth it cannot possibly achieve. That audience may be crowded into the Carrier Dome, Pauley Pavilion, the noisy bowl at Thurber's Ohio State, or be sitting wherever it has chosen in a half empty college gymnasium or stadium. It may have dined on catered meals in comfortable suites at Neyland Stadium or on hot dogs cooked on the makeshift student grills surrounding the open field at Sewanee, Tennessee. And on departure, all will respond with pleasure or regret that this team or that one lost, and thousands will, once the lights are out, place the game in the perspective it deserves, refusing to pursue extravagant and egocentric interpretations of its meaning—a direction, as we have seen, in which infractions may lie.

For those thousands, the residue of their three-hour presence will not be simply the memory of the game as a diversionary amusement. For within the rules under which the game has been played—like those laws and ethical constraints that surround our daily existence—they will have witnessed, and enjoyed, a display of human possibility and error, of continual encounters with the unexpected. And they will have been able to tolerate, even to accommodate, the interminable but somewhat vain intrusions of the coach— calling time, sending directions—to alter this state of affairs. The game cannot, of course, be for those of us present in that audience a complete figure for life: it is too intense, too relentless, not sufficiently meandering or occasional in its disclosures (we must go to the other side of the institutional house for that). But in its self-containment, in its projection of limitation and freedom within a dynamic though temporal relationship, the game has been no less than a brief image of our own human integrity, an image we can carry outside the stadium as we take up again the disordered trivia and statistical forms of daily experience.

We had best take such revelatory encounters where we can find them, even though they emerge from unlikely places. And though we may not fully understand, beyond their entertainment and populist dimensions, the rather mysterious and perhaps even profound evolution of college sports within the national imagination, there seems to be no indication that Americans wish to escape their spell. If the silent meanings of that spell are threatened, obscured by the exploitation of student-athletes, or by the peril of things democratic to become attenuated, commercialized, to become so much like everything else that they lose their connection with our ideals, then it is we who are the losers. For, after all, in our common life, each of us is an amateur. And in the extension of that life into the world of intercollegiate games, we should not have to wonder in whose name the violent maneuvers are being acted out by the young athletes on the green field below, or in whose name the ball is first passed over the shining floor.

NOTE

1. Christopher Lasch, "The I's Have It for Another Decade," *New York Times* (December 27, 1989), p. A23.

INDEX

Substance abuse, deterrence of, 90–92
Symbiosis, 35, 65

T

Telander, Rick, 17 *n.* 5
Tenure for coaches, 83
Thelin, John R., and Lawrence L.
    Wiseman, 108 *n.* 2
Thurber, James, 52
Tobacco, harmful effects, 90
Trust, 101
Tuchman, Barbara, 14, 16, 137
Twain, Mark, 3

U

Universities identified
  Alabama, 42
  Brown, 124
  California, Los Angeles (Pauley
      Pavilion), 140
  Harvard, 47
  Illinois, 52
  Michigan, 3, 42
  Notre Dame, 13
  Ohio State, 52, 140
  Pennsylvania, 47
  Seton Hall, 3
  South (Sewanee), 140
  Swarthmore, 47
  Syracuse (Carrier Dome), 140
  Tennessee (Neyland Stadium), 140
  U. S. Military Academy (West
      Point), 12
  U. S. Naval Academy (Annapolis), 12

Yale, 3, 7, 47
University governance, 41–42, 45, 61
University governing board
    involvement in abuses, 24, 44–45
    proper role of, xiv, 67, 71–73
University president (CEO)
    as physician, 71
    average tenure, 67
    certification of institutional eligibil-
        ity, 31, 73
    compromised authority, 44–45
    key figure in control of athletics,
        41–42, 66–67
    proper role of, 66–71
    quotations, 17 *n.* 6
    relationship with faculty, 74–75
    responsibility for control, 21, 67, 99

V

Victorian England, sportsmanship in, 2

W

Watergate, 14
Weisbrod, Burton A., 5 *n.* 17
White House Conference for a Drug
    Free America, 91
Whitman, Walt, 2, 3
    Leaves of Grass, 2
Wholeness of athletics and academe,
    xiv, 136
Wilson, Robert, 111 *n.* 22
Winning
    emphasis on, 15
    redefinition, 80
Woolf, Virginia, 3, 4, 8, 13